quadrille

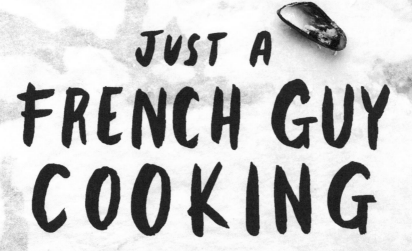

JUST A
FRENCH GUY
COOKING

ALEXIS GABRIEL AÏNOUZ

**Easy recipes and
kitchen hacks for rookies**

Photography by Dan Jones

Foreword

It's such a joy to be writing the foreword to my good mate Alex's beautiful book. We first met when I was looking for a fresh Food Tube star to join the family a few years ago, and as soon as I saw Alex's 'French Guy Cooking' videos I knew we'd discovered a hidden gem. Since then, Alex's channel has become super-successful. And he still cracks me up every time we cook together!

Alex's food is fantastically fun. It's simple but delicious, and always delivered in his brilliantly quirky way. He's a self-taught genius, and he knows exactly what home cooks really want to make. You can't watch him in the kitchen without smiling, and that's what the recipes in this lovely book are all about.

From the French treats you might expect, like the cheat's croissants and the epic 'magic-crust' quiche Lorraine to delights such as ramen four ways and street lamb shish kebab, Alex gets to the heart of joyful, happy cooking. For me, these recipes tick all the big boxes: simple, exciting and ultimately 'eat-me' food!

It's food to spark the imagination of beginner and pro cooks alike, with lovely chatter and helpful tips from Alex running throughout. And with the step-by-step pics, too... well, you can't go wrong!

So guys, turn the page, dive into this bright and colourful collection of gorgeous dishes, and start choosing what you're going to have for dinner! I've got a feeling you'll come back to this lovely book time and time again.

Alex, what can I say mate? You've absolutely nailed it. It's a beaut.

Jamie Oliver

"Salut" guys and thank you for getting my book! Remember: my recipes are here to inspire you and bring you confidence but they need a chef to cook them... that's YOU!

Alex

Eggs

Cheeky shakshuka

Just writing this recipe makes my mouth water. It's the combination of the freshness of the tomato, the umami of the tomato purée, the sweetness of the peppers, the smoothness of the onions, the kick of the harissa and the decadence of the egg running over everything at the end that I find totally irresistible.

Serves 4

a little olive oil
2 onions, chopped
2 merguez sausages or, if not available, 225g [8oz] chorizo, cut into small pieces
2 red and 2 green [bell] peppers, deseeded and thinly sliced
4 ripe tomatoes, cut into strips
1 Tbsp tomato purée [paste]
1 tsp harissa (personally I add 1 Tbsp)
4 garlic cloves, crushed
salt and pepper
4 eggs

Heat a non-stick sauté pan or deep frying pan [skillet] over a medium heat, add a little olive oil and fry the onions and pieces of merguez or chorizo. Once the onions are soft and lightly golden, add the peppers and tomatoes.

Stir in the tomato purée and harissa. Pour in 225ml [1 cup] hot water and add the crushed garlic. Season with salt and pepper.

Cover the pan and leave to cook for about 10 minutes. If necessary, add an extra 115ml [½ cup] water.

Once the sauce has thickened, make 4 indentations in the mixture with the back of a ladle and crack an egg into each. Cover the pan and cook for 2 minutes or until the eggs are done just how you like them.

Harissa – storebought or homemade?

Good harissa certainly has a spicy taste but is also sweet and well balanced. It is a beautiful, brilliant red colour and is not at all bitter. So, if the only harissa you can find in your local supermarket is not up to scratch, make it yourself. To do this, remove the stalks from a handful of mild red chillies and blitz them to a paste with 3 garlic cloves, 1 tsp salt and a pinch of ground coriander. Keep in a jar in the refrigerator, covered with olive oil.

You've-been-doing-it-all-wrong scrambled eggs

I have nothing against traditional scrambled eggs that consist more or less of eggs stirred fairly aggressively in a red-hot saucepan so they spin round a few times. Accompanied with some scorched bacon, they do the job! However, there are also mornings when you'd like to wake up in a luxurious, palatial bedroom and eat a huge posh breakfast. Here is the recipe – expensive – for just those mornings.

Serves 1

3 organic eggs
1 Tbsp very cold butter,
   diced into small pieces
salt and pepper

<u>Serving suggestions</u>
1 Tbsp chopped smoked salmon
   trimmings
1 slice of toast, buttered
1 tsp finely chopped fresh chives
1 tsp salmon roe

Place a saucepan over medium heat and fill it one-third with hot water.

Break the eggs into a heatproof bowl that has a rounded base and is wider than the saucepan. Sit the bowl on top of the saucepan, making sure the boiling water doesn't touch the bottom of the bowl.

Stir constantly, ideally moving your spatula in a figure-of-eight motion, until the mixture thickens. At this point, add the butter to stop the eggs cooking any more and to make them a bit creamy and glossy. Season with salt and pepper.

If you wish, you can also add 1 tablespoon of finely chopped smoked salmon and 1 teaspoon of finely chopped chives at the same time as the butter, mixing them in well. Remove from the heat, spoon onto a slice of buttered toast, and top with 1 teaspoon of salmon roe (and more chives, if you like).

Omelette, Pépin-style

Jacques Pépin is a French celebrity chef who for a long time has been an icon in the US. Very talented, a bit cheeky and with an accent you can cut with a knife (don't look at me!), he is particularly famous for his incomparable omelettes.
This is my take on how he makes them.

Serves 1

3 eggs
pinch of fine salt
a drizzle of neutral flavoured oil
1 tsp butter

Equipment you must have
non-stick frying pan [skillet],
    22–24cm [9–10in] in diameter
a wooden spoon

First of all, beat the eggs, but only lightly as they must not be frothy. Add a pinch of fine salt.

Place a frying pan over a medium-high heat and add the oil and butter. If you cook the omelette over a low heat, it will be solid and cooked evenly all the way through. It's also important to add just enough fat to the pan so the omelette fries but doesn't brown. The mix of oil and butter should 'sing' when it comes into contact with the pan, but not 'scream'.

Pour the eggs into the pan. Shake the pan from front to back holding the handle with your left hand

and, with your right hand, use the wooden spoon to stir the eggs in a circular movement (I'm right-handed). The flecks of cooked egg that progressively appear allow the heat to be distributed throughout the omelette and not just remain at the bottom. Gently pull the sides towards the centre.

When the omelette starts to set, i.e. there is almost no liquid egg left in the pan, tilt the pan away from the handle and carefully roll the omelette over itself using the spoon. By tapping the handle lightly but firmly with the palm of your hand, you'll release the omelette and it will go to the back of the pan. At this point you can add a filling (cheese, ham, etc...) or just fold it over.

Change to holding the handle of the pan with the palm underneath facing upwards and turn out the omelette onto a plate, lifting the plate and tilting it with your right hand. The omelette should be plump and shaped like a half moon.

Making my body remember

Every Saturday lunchtime for about a year, I made an omelette at home. Sometimes with a filling, sometimes without, but always trying to improve my technique. Smoother, more pointed, less golden, more golden, lightly cooked, more cooked... all because I wanted my body and not my head to remember the movements necessary to achieve success. And, also, because without doubt I'm mad.

4 omelettes

An omelette is rather like a blank canvas that you can imagine painting on in a thousand and one ways. But, to be a little more down to earth, an omelette is basically a very efficient way of giving a new lease of life to ingredients that have been sitting around in the refrigerator for a bit too long...

Cheese omelette

When you are ready to roll the omelette over itself, fill the centre with grated cheese. Ideally, use a mix of different types of cheese, such as a mild one that melts easily, like Emmental or mozzarella, and a strong one such as Parmesan, Cheddar or Comté.

Cheat's tortilla

Heat a couple of tablespoons of olive oil in a frying pan [skillet] and add a crushed garlic clove and a finely chopped onion. When the onion becomes translucent, add some leftover, chopped boiled potatoes. Season with salt and pepper and fry for a few minutes.

For a 24-cm [9-in] frying pan, you will need about 5 eggs. Beat the eggs vigorously and pour them into the pan. Cook for 5–10 minutes until the eggs are set and are golden brown underneath and then upturn the omelette out of the pan onto a large plate. Wipe out the pan with kitchen paper [paper towel] and heat 1 tablespoon of olive oil in it. Slide the omelette off the plate back into the pan and leave it to cook until it is evenly golden brown on both sides.

Omelette *aux fines herbes*

The '*fines herbes*' are four in number – fresh parsley, chives, chervil and tarragon. Or, rather, that's the ideal combination but use what you have. Chop the herbs as finely as possible without bruising them (a very sharp knife will make this job a lot easier) and add them to the eggs before you beat them, so the herbs are evenly distributed throughout. Pour the eggs into the pan, cook until just set and then fold the omelette in half before sliding it out of the pan onto a serving plate.

Cheat's *omurice* (Japanese stuffed omelette)

Heat a little oil in a wok or frying pan [skillet] and fry leftover rice with a roughly chopped onion until the rice is lightly golden. Add whatever seafood you have to hand such as crab, prawns [shrimp] or canned tuna and stir for a minute or two to mix it into the rice. Take the pan off the heat and add some chopped chives and 1–2 teaspoons of light soy sauce.

Beat 3 eggs together. Heat a little oil in a 26–28-cm [10–11-in] frying pan and pour in the eggs. The idea is to cook the eggs until they are set in a thin omelette and then spoon the rice mixture into the centre. Fold in the sides towards the centre, doing your best to shape the omelette into an almond – an oval that is slightly pointed at each end.

Crisp-fried eggs, Thai-style

This takes fried eggs to a whole new level but, at the same time, doesn't lose sight of what a simple dish they really are.

Serves 1

3 Tbsp neutral flavoured oil, such as rapeseed
2 large free-range eggs
2 Tbsp Thai sweet chilli sauce
1 tsp light soy sauce
a squeeze of lime juice
1 tsp toasted sesame seeds
leaves from ¼ bunch of fresh coriander [cilantro], mint or basil
½ red or green chilli, sliced into very thin rings

Heat the oil in a frying pan [skillet] – see my cooking tip below – over a high heat until it starts to smoke.

Crack in the eggs and fry them for 2–3 minutes until the whites have become crisp and golden around the edges but the yolks remain runny. Lower the heat.

Divide the chilli sauce and soy sauce between the eggs and baste them with the oil in the pan so the flavours are well mixed together.

Remove the eggs from the pan and serve with the lime juice squeezed over and sprinkled with the sesame seeds, herb leaves and chilli rings.

COOKING TIP

For best results, use a small, heavy-based frying pan. The level of oil will be higher in a small pan so the eggs will fry rapidly and the whites become really crisp. Also, the eggs will look good as they will be neat and round when cooked.

Picture-perfect eggs meurette

A traditional dish made with a sauce from Burgundy that, without doubt, has THE most traditional cuisine in France, which incidentally is THE most traditional country when it comes to cooking. And ME, what do I do? I cheat the thing. Am I crazy? Perhaps... but what the hell, it's so good!

Serves 4

2 glasses of full-bodied red wine
350ml [1½ cups] beef stock
1 Tbsp brown sugar
1 Tbsp oil
6 small shallots or the white parts
   of spring onions [scallions], halved
175g [6oz] lardons
175g [6oz] button mushrooms,
   quartered
2 Tbsp butter mashed with 1 Tbsp
   plain [all-purpose] flour
salt and pepper
a dash of vinegar
4 mega-fresh eggs
5 slices of bread
1 large garlic clove, halved
a few chive stems

WHY PICTURE PERFECT?

The traditional recipe tells you to mix the sauce with the toppings and also to poach the eggs in the wine. That sounds fine, but if I'd made it like that for the photograph, you'd have been disgusted and never, ever tried the dish. #babyvomit

Put the wine and stock in a saucepan over a medium heat, add the sugar and simmer until the liquid has reduced by half. If you want to have a bit of fun (and you know how to do this sort of thing safely), flambé the wine.

In the meantime, heat the oil in a pan and fry the halved shallots or spring onions, the lardons and mushrooms for about 10 minutes.

When the wine and stock have reduced, whisk in the butter and flour mixture until you have a smooth and shiny sauce. Season with salt and pepper. Taste and adjust the seasoning, if necessary.

Bring a saucepan of water, with a dash of vinegar added, to a gentle boil. Break 1 egg into a ramekin and slide it gently into the water. Repeat with the other 3 eggs and leave to cook for 3 minutes, turning the eggs over carefully. Drain the eggs from the pan using a slotted spoon and place on a sheet of kitchen paper [paper towel].

Toast the bread slices. Rub 1 slice with the cut sides of the garlic clove and cut into small croûtons. Place an egg on top of each of the remaining slices and spoon over the onions, lardons, mushrooms, the sauce and the croûtons. Snip some chives into short lengths with scissors, scatter a few on top of each serving – and that's it!

4 eggs en cocotte

I've always found that baking something in the oven impresses guests far more than cooking it in a pan on the hob. It's more 'chef-like'... Bizarre, hey? To give you an example: if you cook an egg en cocotte in a pan, everyone will think it's good but nobody will exclaim "wow". Whereas do it in the oven...

With cheese

Butter small, individual ovenproof dishes and put a little grated cheese in the bottom of each, hollowing the centres to make a nest.

Break an egg into each nest, trying to centre the yolk as much as possible so that it stays nice and runny.

Add 2 teaspoons of crème fraîche to each, 1 teaspoon either side of the yolk, and sprinkle some grated cheese on top.

Preheat the oven to 200°C/180°C fan/400°F/ Gas 6, bake the eggs for 10 minutes – and that's it!

With mushrooms

Finely chop a shallot and coarsely chop some mushrooms. Fry them in a little butter in a pan over a medium heat for 7 minutes, seasoning with salt and pepper.

Put 2 tablespoons of the shallot and mushroom mixture into each individual ovenproof dish, crack in an egg and top with 1 teaspoon of cream. Sprinkle over some grated Comté or Cheddar cheese and bake in the preheated oven as described above.

With kimchi

Dry-fry a bit of bacon in a frying pan [skillet] and, just before it's cooked, add some kimchi. Take the pan off the heat and coarsely chop the bacon and kimchi. Use this mixture as a base for your new-look eggs en cocotte, dividing it between individual ovenproof dishes and hollowing the centres. Crack an egg into each dish and, as well as grated cheese, sprinkle a few chopped chives or spring onions [scallions] on top. Bake as described before.

Like a carbonara

If you have any leftover bacon, chop it roughly with some cooked pasta. Mix together with freshly ground black pepper, a little cream and grated Parmesan. Spoon into individual ovenproof dishes and hollow out the centres. Crack in the eggs, dust with grated Parmesan and bake as described before.

#HACK

Wine pairing for dummies (aka normal people)

Let's be clear – I have never smelt 'smoked-crystallized-fruits-from-the-undergrowth-on-a-bed-of-fresh-moss' when drinking a glass of wine. Never, ever. Personally, I've just enjoyed it and, according to the top oenologists, that's how you appreciate wine.

Having said that, choosing the right wine can sometimes be a bit of a minefield and, if you don't want to go beyond what you enjoy, I'd advise you to drink wine the same colour as the food you're eating. It's weird but it works pretty well.

However, if you do want to get into it more deeply, here is the simple method I follow each time I'm choosing a wine: in my head, I have a classification of dishes ranging from the most delicate to the most intensely flavoured. This reads something like: raw food, seafood, starters, vegetable dishes, fish, white meat, red meat, spicy dishes, sweet things/desserts.

Now here is a classification of wines also going from the lightest to the heaviest: dry white (Muscadet, Sauvignon Blanc) or rosé, full-bodied white (Chardonnay) or rosé, light red (Gamay, Pinot Noir), medium red (Merlot, Sangiovese), full-bodied red (Zinfandel, Shiraz/Syrah) plus sweet wines (Sauternes) and super-aromatic wines (Gewürztraminer).

All that remains is to put these two classifications alongside each other and you'll have a pretty efficient way of picking the right wine to go with a dish. For example:

Seafood – dry white (a good beer is even better but that's just me)

Salad – dry white

Raw vegetables – light to full-bodied white or light red

Chicken – full-bodied white or light red

Roasted vegetables – medium red

Beef, lamb – full-bodied red

Indian curry – super-aromatic white

Black Forest gâteau – sweet wine

Of course, like every rule in the world, this one is to be taken with a pinch of salt. Sometimes you'll find that a red wine goes well with a dessert and it would be a shame to deprive yourself. (Personally, I love red wine with chocolate but I'd never admit it publicly.)

What about cheese?

Many people (including French ones) picture a glass of red wine complementing an oozing Camembert. Well... it's difficult to be more wrong. Instead, go for a dry white wine as its freshness will 'cut through' the fat, salt and cream in the cheese.

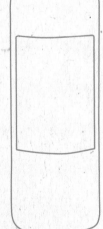

Soups

MY THING

Something I really like
is to add cold pesto to
a hot soup as I find the
contrast really brings out
the fantastic aroma of
the basil (or whichever
herb you've used).

An open-minded soupe au pistou

This vegetarian soup is how they make minestrone in Provence. As we're being a bit open-minded, instead of ordinary basil you'll find the pistou is equally good made with Thai basil, tarragon, coriander (cilantro) or even mint (in which case use only one-third mint to two-thirds parsley). You can also be creative with your choice of cheese, so instead of grated Parmesan, try another variety such as Comté or mature Cheddar.

Serves 4

2 garlic cloves
pinch of sea [kosher] salt flakes
1 bunch of fresh basil
3 Tbsp extra virgin olive oil
50g [½ cup] grated Parmesan
1 carrot
1 courgette [zucchini]
2 red tomatoes (want to use yellow ones? Sounds a super idea to me)
2 sprigs of fresh thyme
2 bay leaves
about 2L [8½ cups] vegetable stock or water
100g [3½oz] frozen green beans
100g [½ cup] frozen peas
400g (14oz) can cannellini beans, drained and rinsed

And finally

By adding some small pasta shapes to the soup (orzo, elbow, etc), you can turn it into a complete meal.

To make the *pistou* (which is actually just pesto without any nuts), peel 1 of the garlic cloves, place it in a pestle and mortar or small food processor and add the salt. Crush the garlic and then add the basil leaves a few at a time, grinding them until you have a paste. Mix in the olive oil a little at a time until evenly combined, as if you were making mayonnaise, and finally add the grated cheese.

Slice the remaining garlic clove. Cut the carrot, courgette and tomatoes into equal-sized small cubes, measuring less than 1cm [⅜in].

Put the carrot, sliced garlic, thyme and bay leaves in a large saucepan and pour in the vegetable stock or water. Leave to simmer over a medium heat until the stock or water has reduced by one third.

After 10 minutes add the courgette, green beans and peas. After 20 minutes add the tomatoes and after 30 minutes the drained cannellini beans. Simmer until the beans are heated through. Taste and adjust the seasoning as necessary.

A little piece of advice: avoid stirring as the vegetables will become mushy and you risk the soup becoming very cloudy. Also avoid adding seasoning too early – in other words before the cooking liquid has reduced – as the finished soup risks being much too salty.

Spoon a good ladleful into each soup bowl and add a generous spoonful of *pistou* in the centre. Leave diners to swirl the two together as then they'll feel they've had a hand in making the soup (which, between ourselves, isn't the case as you're the chef).

Pot-au-pho-bò

This is speed dating between a comforting French pot-au-feu and a fragrant and exotic Vietnamese pho bo soup. It is, I think, a poor imitation of a classic pot-au-feu, just as it would be scandalous to claim it as authentic Vietnamese cuisine, but at the end of the day it works rather well. So there!

Serves 4

For the bouillon
2 large yellow or white onions, unpeeled
5-cm [2-in] piece of root ginger, unpeeled and roughly sliced
1 Tbsp oil
100g [3½oz] minced [ground] beef
salt and pepper
2 beef marrow bones (if unavailable, a chicken carcass would work)
1 beef stock cube, crumbled
1 leek, trimmed and cut into 5-cm [2-in] lengths
2 Tbsp fish sauce
3–4 sprigs of thyme and 2 bay leaves tied together
3 large pinches of five-spice powder (or, if you're feeling adventurous, roast 4 whole cloves with 2 star anise, 2 cinnamon sticks and 2 tsp coriander seeds and grind together to make your own)

To serve
2 carrots
1 celery stick
4 vermicelli rice noodle nests
400g [14oz] beef carpaccio or, if you're looking for a challenge, a piece of steak cut into wafer-thin slices (the freezer is your friend here as, if the steak is really cold, it will be easier to slice very finely)
Thai basil or ordinary basil
Coriander [cilantro]

Cut the onions in half and grill [broil] them, cut side down, with the ginger, until nicely charred but not completely black – grilling the onions and ginger will add colour to the stock. If you have a gas cooker you can do this over a flame on the hob. But beware: flames + fingers = problems, somewhere I don't want to go.

Heat the oil in a large, deep saucepan, season the minced beef with salt and pepper and sear it over a high heat for 2 minutes. Add the marrow bones (or chicken carcass), the stock cube, onion halves, ginger, leeks, fish sauce, thyme and bay leaves.

Pour in 3 litres [3 quarts] of water, bring to the boil, lower the heat and simmer for 30 minutes.

To serve, use a speed [swivel] peeler to shave the carrots and celery into thin strips and then cut these into fine matchsticks (about 10cm [4in] long).

Put a vermicelli nest in each serving bowl and strain the bouillon into the bowls. If you've used beef bones, scoop out the marrow from the bones into the bowls and add the leeks as well.

Garnish with slices of raw beef and the carrot and celery shavings. Finish with the basil and coriander – and slurp.

Soup mash-up

Pot-au-feu is a richly flavoured clear bouillon in which different vegetables and chunks of meltingly tender beef gently float. In Vietnamese pho soup, the accent is not on vegetables but on a balance between clear and spicy (cinnamon, star anise...) bouillon and tender beef, sliced very thinly.

'Sort of' ayam

I tasted my first Indonesian Soto Ayam in a London street in the pouring rain on a freezing cold day. Believe me, it was a taste of sunshine.

Serves 4

4 chicken thighs, skinned
salt and pepper
1 lemongrass stalk, bashed
    and tied in a knot
a pinch of ground turmeric
600ml [2½ cups] coconut milk
600ml [2½ cups] chicken stock
2 garlic cloves, skinned and crushed
2.5-cm [1-in] piece of root ginger,
    peeled and grated
4 nests of dried rice vermicelli

For the toppings
1 lime, quartered
1 hard-boiled egg, peeled
    and quartered
prawn crackers
fried shallots
dried chilli flakes
chopped fresh aromatic herbs –
    use whatever you have available
    such as coriander [cilantro], celery
    leaves, parsley, mint... it doesn't
    matter

Cut 3 or 4 deep slashes in each chicken thigh and season them generously with salt and pepper.

Put the thighs in a large saucepan and add the lemongrass, turmeric, coconut milk, chicken stock, garlic and ginger. Simmer over a low heat for about 30 minutes and then remove and discard the lemongrass.

Lift out the chicken thighs and take the meat off the bones. Place a vermicelli nest in each serving bowl and pour over the piping hot cooking liquid. Add the boned chicken pieces and serve garnished with the toppings.

A crash course in ramen

I have a confession to make: I just love instant ramen. I know that sounds terrible, especially coming from someone who tells people what – and what not – to eat and who tries (not always successfully, though) to set an example. The truth is, I can't help it. I just enjoy the savoury kick I get every time I split open a pack of noodles.

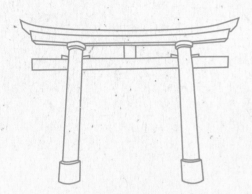

For the ultimate experience, it is necessary to follow the five successive Japanese gates called torii. Torii, 鳥居, literally means a dwelling place for birds and is pronounced *to.ri.i* in Japanese. This traditional gate is most commonly found at the entrance to a Shinto shrine, or within it, where it symbolizes the transition from the mundane to the sacred.

The gate of the Broth – the foundation

Packed with umami, it can be rich or light, cloudy or clear, and pork-, chicken- or seafood-based, or even made with a combination of them. It's often combined with dashi, a broth made from dried, smoked bonito flakes and sea kelp.

The gate of the Noodles – the structure

Without noodles, it's not ramen. They are alkaline noodles, or to be more precise, often made from wheat flour with a low hydration content.

The gate of the Toppings – the texture

Chasu braised pork, marinated soft-boiled egg (*ajitsuke tamago*), spring onions [scallions], nori seaweed, *menma* fermented bamboo shoots and even sweet corn. They bring colour and different textures to the soup.

The gate of *Tare* – the salt

The flavouring base which is usually one of the following: *shio* (salt), *shoyu* (soy sauce) or *miso* (fermented soya bean paste).

The gate of Aroma Oil – the fat

This is picked up by the noodles as you slurp them. Common varieties of infused oil are black garlic oil, sesame oil, onion oil... Butter also works very well (I am French, so what do you expect...?).

Once you've mastered the theory, you must practise and there is no better way to do this than to get out there and eat some really good ramen. I'd suggest you at least try:

Tokyo ramen – pork and chicken broth + dashi + curly noodles. Classic.

Sapporo miso ramen – thick noodles + *akamiso* + cabbage, sweet corn and minced pork. Butter is the icing on its cake.

Hakata *tonkotsu* ramen – cloudy and fatty broth made from pork bones, sesame and black garlic oil. Intensely flavoured.

4 four ways to instantly upgrade ramen

My guilty secret is I'm addicted to instant Chinese-style noodles. I'm trying to give them up but while I'm waiting to be cured, I might as well have another fix. So, here are four almost instant combinations of ingredients that will add colour and flavour to the stock you use to cook the noodles. Most of the ingredients are added as toppings just before serving.

To add to instant beef-flavoured ramen
Thai basil and/or coriander [cilantro]
bean sprouts
thin slices of raw beef
small piece of star anise and cinnamon stick (added to the cooking liquid for the noodles)

To add to instant pork-flavoured ramen
corn kernels
chopped spring onions [scallions]
a drizzle of milk and/or a knob of butter
fried bacon bits (add when the noodles are almost cooked)

To add to instant onion-flavoured ramen
shredded young spinach leaves
grated fresh root ginger
a soft-boiled egg
a few drops of sesame oil

To add to instant vegetarian ramen
minced mushrooms
shredded Chinese cabbage
   (add when the noodles are
   almost cooked)
carrots cut into matchsticks
   (add with the cabbage)
fried tofu

Baguette ball soup

Serves 4

stale bread, preferably baguette
2 Tbsp neutral flavoured oil,
    e.g. rapeseed [canola],
    groundnut [peanut]
½ onion, finely chopped
leftover roast chicken bones and skin
4 large eggs
½ tsp baking powder
1 litre [4 cups] well-flavoured
    chicken stock
salt and pepper
225g [8oz] cooked chicken
2 carrots
2 sticks of celery
chopped fresh dill or thyme leaves

Blitz the bread in a food processor until turned into fine crumbs – you will need 125g [1⅔ cups]. Set aside.

Heat the oil over a medium-low heat in a frying pan [skillet], add the chopped onion and the chicken bones and skin and fry gently for 10–15 minutes, stirring from time to time. Pass the contents of the pan through a fine strainer to separate the oil from the other ingredients, reserving the oil.

Put the eggs, breadcrumbs, baking powder, the drained oil infused with the onion and chicken and 4 tablespoons of the chicken stock into a large bowl. Season with salt and pepper and mix everything together thoroughly. Chill in the refrigerator for 15 minutes.

With damp hands, shape the breadcrumb mixture into small, walnut-sized balls. Put on a plate or board in a single layer and chill the matzo balls for 1 hour to firm them up.

Heat a saucepan of salted water until simmering, add the matzo balls and poach them over a medium-low heat, with the pan covered, for about 30 minutes.

Cut the chicken, carrots and celery into small pieces and microwave the vegetables on full power for 2 minutes to cook them.

Reheat the remaining the stock and ladle it into 4 soup bowls. Divide the matzo balls between the bowls of steaming stock and add the pieces of chicken, carrots and celery. Scatter over the herbs and serve.

At home, I've always got some leftover
baguette hanging around from the night before.
For me, buying a baguette is the norm as it's good,
not expensive and available on every street corner in
Paris. However, having seen the price of a baguette
abroad, I'd guess if you bought one where you live,
it wouldn't have time to go stale, so for this recipe
use whatever bread you have to hand.

A convenient onion soup

You simply can't ignore French 'soupe à l'oignon'. I agree it looks gorgeous served in those pretty round bowls but, one: it takes a lot of preparation; and two: it makes a lot of washing up, so it's not very practical, I'm sure you'll agree.

Serves 6

1 Tbsp butter
1 Tbsp neutral flavoured oil, such as rapeseed
6 large onions, thinly sliced
salt
1 Tbsp brown sugar
200ml [scant 1 cup] dry white wine
3 Tbsp any type of cognac (prefer to use rum or vodka? That's OK, but choose an amber-coloured one)
1 Tbsp flour
2 litres [8½ cups] good-quality beef or vegetable stock
½ garlic clove
slices of stale bread
100–150g [1–1½ cups] grated hard cheese (Comté, strong Cheddar)

Put a large, heavy-based saucepan over a medium-low heat, add the butter and oil and then the onions. Season with salt and add the sugar. Leave to cook for 30 minutes, stirring from time to time – the onions must be golden brown.

Pour in the wine, then the cognac, and flambé (watch out for the flames when doing this). When the flames have died down, scrape the bottom of the saucepan with a wooden spoon to incorporate all the cooking juices sticking to it. Stir in the flour – this will give the soup a rich, syrupy consistency.

Mix well and then add the stock. Turn down the heat as low as it will go and leave to simmer for 30 minutes.

Rub a large gratin dish with the garlic and pour in the soup. Cover the surface with bread slices and top them with a generous layer of grated cheese.

Grill [broil] until the cheese bubbles and turns a nice golden brown before placing the dish triumphantly in the centre of the table. The heat and steam are fierce enough to burn the table cloth, which admittedly would add considerably to the drama, but if you're attached to the cloth, put a trivet or pot stand on the table first.

NOTE!

I'm giving you a classic, fuss-free version of onion soup here but, if you're after more complex flavours, add a pinch of mixed spice and a bouquet garni before starting to simmer the soup.

Salads

#HACK

6 fresh herbs

I always buy these fragrant herbs fresh, as, for me, they are so delicate and fragile they lose almost all their appeal when they are dried. One piece of advice – you should avoid cooking them as you'll destroy their flavour and aroma.

Parsley A fairly strong herb that adds freshness and substance to a dish. I always use the Italian flat-leaf variety as it's more aromatic.

Food pairing: mussels, chicken, bulgur wheat, liver, butter, lemon, garlic

Coriander [cilantro]
Delicate but pungent, this is a double-edged herb! I adore its lemon and undeniably Asian and Eastern aroma but some people detest it.

Food pairing: pork, chilli, crab, lemongrass, pineapple, cucumber, avocado

Chive This has a lovely flavour, which reminds you of the best bits of onions and garlic. If you don't have any, use the green parts of spring onions [scallions].

Food pairing: dumplings, lobster, eggs, calamari, mushrooms, butter, lettuce

Mint Fresh, with a menthol kick, this is a powerful herb. Use it sparingly as you can ruin a dish if you add too much. Use it quickly as the leaves go black easily and will spoil other herbs that come into contact with it.

Food pairing: hummus, melon, lentils, feta, lamb, peas, coconut

Dill

With its slight aniseed flavour, delicate dill, used in Scandinavian cuisine, is reminiscent of fennel.

Food pairing: pickled veg, eggs, salmon, cream, yogurt, cauliflower

Basil Along with oregano, this herb really makes me think of Italy. It has a marvellous freshness (more delicate than mint) with hints of aniseed and lemon.

Food pairing: pasta, peanuts, mango, strawberries, courgettes [zucchini], spicy beef

And as a bonus – chervil

More subtly flavoured than parsley, with less aniseed than tarragon but as delicate and fragile as dill, chervil is perhaps my favourite fresh herb in French cuisine.

#HACK
6 dried herbs

Thyme, rosemary, oregano, and other herbs that grow in hot climates, all retain their aroma extremely well when dried. They can also be stored for much longer than when they are fresh so are very practical in the kitchen. Here is my herbal dream team.

Thyme Those super-small, pointy leaves have a pungent but fresh aroma that's slightly tangy, almost citrusy, reminding me of lemons, oranges and lemongrass. Thyme is a staple part of Mediterranean and Middle Eastern cuisines.

Food pairing: black peppercorns, steak, bone marrow, garlic, chicken, figs, potatoes, any roasted vegetables

Bay leaf Ideal for marinades as its aroma reminds me of two things – the enormous bay bush in my grandmother's garden, and Coca Cola. Life is strange, isn't it? A word of advice, remove the bay leaf after cooking, as you can't eat it.

Food pairing: osso buco, any stew, pears, white wine, honey, chickpeas, soups, sauces

Rosemary Stronger than thyme, rosemary's silvery needle-like leaves are also firmer so it's necessary to chop the leaves more finely or, if using whole sprigs, remove them after a dish is cooked. Rosemary is also brilliant in a marinade.

Food pairing: lamb, olives, peaches, new potatoes, [bell] peppers, almonds

Oregano When I think of this herb, I think pizza. Bunches of oregano hanging by their stalks make great decorations in my kitchen (it's me who does the housework!).

Food pairing: tomatoes, pizza (marinara being the quintessential example), yogurt, spicy dishes, black beans

Sage This has a distinctive flavour and I'd have trouble eating it raw as it's too strong for me. However, when it's cooked or fried, sage enhances many dishes with its unique character and flavour.

Food pairing: gnocchi, onions, squash, polenta, rabbit, sausages, wheat, capers

Savory Less well known than the others, which is a pity, because this herb has a wonderful aroma – peppery, spicy, halfway between thyme and garlic... It's said to be an aphrodisiac as well, so it really has everything going for it.

Food pairing: lentils, green beans, broad [fava] beans, chicken, root vegetables

Cold green lentils and Chinese sausage

I've given this bistro classic a new twist by replacing smoked salmon, which the French traditionally use, with smoked Cantonese sausage. The vinaigrette is there to cut through the fattiness of the sausage, bringing the dish to life and making it punchier.

Serves 4

For the salad
300g [1⅔ cups] dried green lentils – I'm being totally objective here when I say that French green lentils are without doubt the best for this dish
4 links of smoked Chinese sausage
6 radishes, sliced into rounds
6 spring onions [scallions], sliced into rounds, keeping the green and white parts separate

For the vinaigrette
3 Tbsp olive oil
1 Tbsp red wine vinegar
1 tsp mustard
a knife point of crushed garlic
salt and pepper

The lentils don't need pre-soaking – just put them in a pan of cold water without any salt and boil for 25 minutes, adding the Chinese sausages after 10 minutes. Drain and leave the lentils and sausages to cool and then chill them in the refrigerator until you're ready to make the salad.

During this time, make the vinaigrette by whisking together all the ingredients, making sure you add the mustard or you won't get a stable emulsion.

In a bowl, mix together the lentils, the sausages cut into rounds, the sliced radishes, the white part of the spring onions and the vinaigrette. Serve with the green part of the onions scattered over.

Did you know?

The Cantonese name for the sausages is Lap Cheong. Since they are dried, cured and smoked, they are usually sold sous vide so will keep for over a year, if unopened. It's super-easy to spot them in an oriental food store as the pack will have 臘腸 written on it – are you OK with that?

Colourful carrot salad

This recipe is inspired by Morocco, whose cuisine is one of north Africa's finest and is certainly one of my favourites. Full of tempting aromas and spices, it often combines sweet and savoury flavours, as it does here.

Serves 4

4 Tbsp natural Greek yogurt
a few drops of orange flower water
a good squeeze of fresh orange juice
1 orange
salt and pepper
6 carrots of different colours,
    or just use orange ones if you
    want (but that's a bit dull!)
chopped pistachios and ground
    cinnamon, for dusting
flat-leaf parsley, to garnish

In a bowl, mix the yogurt with the orange flower water, the orange juice and a little grated zest from the orange (aka the peel). Season with salt and pepper and set to one side.

Cut the carrots lengthwise into very thin ribbons: the easiest way to do this is with a speed [swivel] peeler. Slice the top and bottom off the orange and stand it upright. Using a small sharp knife, cut away the thick skin and pith, starting at the top and cutting down to the base. Remove the segments of orange flesh – they're called 'supremes' – leaving behind the white membranes.

Arrange the carrots and orange segments on a serving plate, lightly drizzle over the yogurt dressing and sprinkle with chopped pistachios and a pinch of ground cinnamon. Garnish with flat-leaf parsley.

REMEMBER!

A speed peeler is totally brilliant for shaving off really thin ribbons. I use it all the time with all kinds of vegetables when I want to give them a whole new identity in salads.

Herring with warm potato salad

Classic stuff, but this recipe teaches you about pairing cold and hot. Definitely one of my favourite starters as it's simple but stylish. The idea behind this classic bistro recipe is to play on the contrast of the hot potato with the cold marinated herring.

Serves 4

4 smoked herring (or kipper) fillets
2 shallots, finely chopped
4 small carrots, sliced into thin rounds
4 sprigs of fresh dill, finely chopped
1 Tbsp whole spices for marinating fish,
　　e.g. fennel seeds, coriander seeds,
　　black or pink peppercorns
3 bay leaves
6 Tbsp neutral flavoured oil –
　　if you have walnut or hazelnut
　　oil in your storecupboard, add
　　a few drops as well
2 Tbsp cider vinegar or white wine
　　vinegar
4 medium-sized potatoes,
　　peeled and left whole

To finish
dill sprigs and shallot slices

An hour before serving, put the herring fillets in a shallow dish with the shallots, carrots, dill, whole spices and bay leaves. Spoon over the oil and vinegar, cover the dish with clingfilm [plastic wrap] and chill in the refrigerator until ready to serve.

Cook the potatoes in a saucepan of boiling water for 20–30 minutes, according to their size, until tender. The classic technique insists you boil the potatoes with their skins on – and then burn your fingers peeling them! So, I peel them first before cooking – sacrilege, I know.

Drain the potatoes, cut them into 5-mm [¼-in] thick slices and arrange on four serving plates. Slice the herrings like smoked salmon, but in thicker slices, and add to the potatoes with the carrots. Scatter with small sprigs of dill and shallot slices and then pour a dash of the marinade over each serving.

Pictures on pages 36, 44 and 45.

Niçoise salad with anchovies, tomatoes, artichokes and broad beans

This salad perfectly sums up the Mediterranean cooking I love so much. It's simple, fresh, seasonal and popular but OH SO controversial. The arguments over the correct way to serve it could probably start a war. One thing everybody does agree on, though, is that cooked stuff should be left out.

Serves 4

6 medium-sized tomatoes
salt
3 eggs
1 green [bell] pepper
4 radishes
2 spring onions [scallions]
1kg [2lb 4oz] young fresh broad [fava]
    bean pods – if you can't find these,
    quickly boil 250g [9oz] frozen broad
    beans *but tell no one*
4 small purple artichokes
1 garlic clove, peeled
12–16 anchovy fillets
olive oil

Start by cutting the tomatoes into wedges. Put the wedges on kitchen paper [paper towels], sprinkle with salt and let them drain for a few minutes. This concentrates the flavour of the tomatoes and makes the finished salad less watery.

Boil the eggs for 8 minutes and then drain and cool them in a bowl of cold water. Peel and cut the eggs into wedges

Remove the stalk from the green pepper and cut into thin, round slices, discarding the core and seeds. Slice the radishes thinly and finely chop the spring onions.

Remove the beans from their pods. When they are young and fresh they are usually fine to eat raw and don't need cooking.

Cut off the artichoke stalks, leaving about 1cm [½in]. Remove any tough outer leaves, trim off the top thirds and cut away any fibrous bits around the base with a small sharp knife. Slice the artichokes in half, remove any hairs and slice them. Drop immediately into a bowl of cold water with a squeeze of lemon juice added to it to stop them discolouring.

Rub a large serving dish with the garlic clove so it gives you a kiss, not a slap. Arrange the tomatoes, eggs, pepper slices, radishes, beans and artichokes in the dish and scatter over the spring onions and anchovies. Serve drizzled with olive oil – there's no need to add vinegar as acidity comes from the salad ingredients.

The poached eggs are
optional but they definitely
add that all important
final flourish to the salad.

Frisée salad with bacon bits, croûtons and a maple syrup dressing

The famous 'frisée aux lardons' – now that's a salad with style! Hot, cold, crunchy, crisp, silky, salty, bitter, sweet... It ticks all the taste bud boxes in one go. And, if you add any cooked potatoes that are left over, you'll have a complete meal.

Serves 4

a little oil for frying
6 bacon rashers [slices], cut into large lardons
½ medium-sized onion, roughly chopped
150g [5oz] stale bread, cut into small cubes (honestly, I never have any stale bread and there's never time to leave it to go stale, so just use the bread you have)
4 eggs (the fresher they are, the easier they will be to poach)
4 Tbsp apple cider vinegar
2 Tbsp maple syrup
8 Tbsp rapeseed or groundnut [peanut] oil
1 tsp Dijon mustard
salt and pepper
1 large frisée lettuce [French curly endive]
chopped fresh chives

If you can't find frisée...

Use another type of salad but choose one with character i.e. bitter and crunchy, as it is crucial for getting the balance of the recipe right. I'd suggest, dandelion leaves (greens), cos (romaine) lettuce, wild chicory (endive)...

Heat a little oil in a frying pan [skillet] over medium heat and fry the bacon lardons, onion and bread cubes. The idea is that these last two get acquainted as soon as they meet.

Heat water in a saucepan until it comes to the boil and then turn the heat down so the water is just simmering gently. Break an egg into a mug and slide it very carefully into the water. Poach for 3–4 minutes and then lift out the egg with a slotted spoon and drain it on kitchen paper [paper towels]. If you're struggling with this, the best YouTube video showing you how to do it is the one by English chef Heston Blumenthal. Repeat with the remaining three eggs.

Put the vinegar, maple syrup, oil, mustard, salt and pepper in a jar. Screw the lid on the jar and shake it well to combine the ingredients and make a smooth, tasty dressing.

Wash and drain the frisée lettuce thoroughly.

Toss the lettuce with the dressing until the leaves are coated and divide them between 4 serving plates. Spoon the bacon, onion and bread cubes on top and sprinkle over the chives. Finally, place a poached egg in the centre of each serving. Leave diners to cut into the eggs so the runny yolks ooze over the salad.

Spring greens coleslaw

This recipe is inspired by the soul food of America's Deep South, where the dishes not only showcase simple local ingredients but they are also made with so much love. To me that's real cooking. Ordinary coleslaw is too rich for me. Despite being lighter, this is still comfort food but with just a hint of soul.

Serves lots of people – it's great for a party

For the dressing
8 Tbsp full-fat yogurt (dairy-free yogurt works fine too)
2 tsp mild mustard (or Dijon if you want the dressing to have more of a kick)
2 Tbsp cider vinegar
salt and pepper

For the coleslaw
300g [10½oz] fresh spring [collard] greens
¼ head of white cabbage
100g [2 cups] soft salad leaves, e.g. baby kale or spinach
100g [2 cups] peppery salad leaves, e.g. watercress, rocket [arugula], dandelion leaves [greens]
1 carrot
2 large apples, cored
400g [3 cups] corn kernels
½ bunch of fresh parsley, chopped

Start by making the dressing. Mix the yogurt with the mustard, add the cider vinegar (just right for this light dressing) and season with salt and pepper. Taste and adjust the flavour according to your taste. I often make this in larger quantities, as it will easily keep in the refrigerator for 5–6 days.

For the coleslaw, slice the greens, cabbage, soft salad and peppery salad finely and grate the carrot and apples. Place the prepared vegetables and fruit, the corn and chopped parsley in a large bowl, pour over the dressing and mix well. I always do this with my hands as I can crush the salad a little at the same time so the dressing permeates the fruit and vegetables and their texture will be softer.

A recommendation

I discovered soul food from a book that I absolutely adore – 'Vibration Cooking: Or, the Travel Notes of a GeeChee Girl' by Vertamae Smart-Grosvenor, who is herself descended from slaves.

Panzanella, or the art of the stale bread salad

This salad means summer to me as it is food that sustains the body and refreshes the mind in equal measure. The inspiration for the salad comes, of course, from Italy but by making it with leftover sourdough bread rather than ciabatta, I get the feeling – mistaken, no doubt – that I'm making it a tiny bit my own.

Serves 2

300g [10½oz] sourdough bread, slightly stale, or – more realistically – a bit past its best
6 tomatoes
½ cucumber
1 green or red [bell] pepper
½ red onion
salt and pepper
1–2 Tbsp red wine vinegar
olive oil
small bunch of fresh basil or tarragon
50g [2oz] pecorino cheese

Cut the bread into 1–2-cm (⅜–¾-in) cubes and, most important, don't throw away any crumbs as they can be used to thicken the dressing.

Cut the tomatoes, cucumber and pepper into pieces of a similar size to the bread.

Chop the onion very finely and plunge it into a bowl of very cold, salted water. This cools the ardour of the onion, making it less hot, and also crisps it up.

In a large salad bowl, mix the red wine vinegar with three times as much olive oil and season with salt and pepper. Add all the chopped ingredients and the reserved breadcrumbs and massage everything together with your hands so the vinaigrette infuses the bread and vegetables.

Finally, shred the basil or tarragon leaves, crumble the pecorino and scatter both over the salad.

A CONFESSION

I always finish by drinking all the juices that have mixed together and formed a 'sauce' at the bottom of the bowl.

My thing

I love making this salad without using a knife. I shred, break and crumble all the ingredients with my hands and then knead them together a little. This gives the salad a very natural look, almost a bit wild, and that relaxes me.

Snacks

Sourdough bread recipe for normal people

This is NOT easy but, in my opinion, it is the easiest sourdough bread recipe out there. So – hey! – that's already got to be a plus!

For the sourdough starter

In a large, clean jar, mix 20g [¾oz] wholemeal [wholewheat] bread flour with 4 teaspoons of tepid, still mineral water. Cover loosely with clingfilm [plastic wrap] and leave in a warm place for 1–3 days. Eventually, tiny bubbles will appear on top. Add 2½ tablespoons of water and 40g [1½oz] wholemeal bread flour. Cover again loosely and leave for 1 day – the mix will rise and fall back again. Add another 80g [3oz] wholemeal bread flour and 80ml [⅓ cup] water. After less than a day, the mix should have risen and have lots of bubbles. Congratulations, you've just given birth to a sourdough starter! Now, every morning, discard all but 2 tablespoons of the starter and add 2 tablespoons of water, and 1 tablespoon each of wholemeal and white bread flour.

To make the sourdough bread

Put 2 tablespoons of sourdough starter in a clean bowl and mix in 100ml [scant ½ cup] tepid water and 100g [¾ cup] white bread flour. Cover and leave in a warm place until doubled in size, and light and foamy (3–5 hours). Now put the mix in a big bowl and add 400ml [1⅓ cups] tepid water and 600g [4½ cups] white bread flour. Mix well, cover and rest for 30 minutes. Add 2 teaspoons of salt and a splash of water and stir. Scrape out the dough onto a work surface and knead vigorously for 10 minutes. You'll think I'm having a laugh but keep kneading and eventually the dough will become elastic, smooth and sticky. Place in a bowl, cover with film and 'prove' in a warm place for 4 hours.

Tip out the dough onto an unfloured work surface, sprinkle with flour and flip it over.

Build up tension by folding the edges of the dough to the centre to make a rough ball. Cover and rest for 30 minutes, during which time it will flatten. Sprinkle the dough with flour, flip over and fold like an envelope – bottom to top, right to left, left to right, top to bottom and then bottom to top again. Finally, roll it up. With the seam underneath, slowly but firmly push the dough out in all directions with the palm of your hand – you should feel the surface tension building up which will give the dough a nice tight surface. Line a large bowl with kitchen paper [paper towels] and dust liberally with rice flour. Shape the dough into a ball and dust it with rice flour as well. Put the dough upside down in the bowl so the seal is uppermost. Dust that with flour, cover the bowl and refrigerate overnight. Two hours before you want to bake the loaf, get the dough out of the refrigerator. If it doesn't spring back when you press it lightly, leave for a few hours more.

Put a cast-iron casserole [Dutch oven] in the oven 30 minutes before baking and preheat the oven to 250°C/475°F/Gas 9. Lay a sheet of parchment paper on the worktop and gently turn the dough out of the bowl upside down onto it. Score the dough lengthwise with a razor blade, held at a low angle, cutting about 1cm [⅜in] deep. Take the casserole out of the oven, lift up the paper and dough, and lower both into the casserole, taking care as the casserole will be very hot.. Put the lid on and whack back in the oven. Immediately lower the temperature to 220°C/425°F/Gas 7 and bake for 25 minutes. Remove the lid and bake for 25 minutes more or until golden brown. Turn out and cool the loaf on a wire rack before slicing.

Two tartines: NYC vs Paris

French cuisine sometimes suffers from the view that it is a bit old-fashioned, snobbish and even up itself (or, as we say over here, 'coincé du cul', if you'll pardon my French). To me, this image needs shaking up when it comes to easy, fun dishes such as tartines, which are open sandwiches and a bit like pizza - right?

Each tartine serves 1

2 large slices of sourdough bread

For the NYC
2–3 Tbsp cream cheese
1 large tomato, diced
2–3 slices of lox (see my note about this below)
1 tsp capers
2 or 3 very thin rings of red onion

For the Paris
2–3 green asparagus spears
2 Tbsp white wine vinegar
1 tsp sugar
salt
1 large garlic clove
lightly salted butter
1–2 slices of good-quality cooked ham
2 red-skinned radishes
fresh chervil leaves (or use parsley, tarragon, thyme)

NOTE

Lox is salmon that has been cured and then cold-smoked and is very popular in the US - particularly as a topping for bagels with cream cheese. You can use smoked salmon equally well but go for fatty slices with white stripes running through them.

Start by toasting or grilling [broiling] the sourdough but only do this lightly as the idea is not to crisp it up like a rusk but rather to prevent it absorbing moisture from the toppings. At the same time, slightly scorched patches are good. I know, I'm making things complicated, but bread is in my DNA.

For the NYC, spread the toasted bread generously with cream cheese and then top with alternate layers of tomato and lox. Sprinkle over the capers and finally add red onion rings.

For the Paris, shave the asparagus spears into thin ribbons using a speed [swivel] peeler and place them in a bowl with the vinegar, sugar and a pinch of salt. Set aside to 'pickle' while you get on with the rest of the recipe.

Slice the radishes into rounds.

Cut the garlic clove in half, rub the cut sides over the toast and then spread with a thin layer of butter. If you don't have lightly salted butter, unsalted will do the job but sprinkle it with sea [kosher] salt flakes.

Ask your butcher or delicatessen to slice your ham very thinly and arrange the slices on the bread so they look like waves (this will add volume).

Drain the asparagus and place on top of the ham with the radishes. Finally, sprinkle with your fresh herbs. Cut the tartine into 3 with a bread knife and serve.

Vegetable spring rolls with sriracha mayonnaise

A super-fresh and super-colourful vegetable take on Vietnamese spring rolls. Those rice wrappers are precious by the way – cheap to buy, they keep forever and can be used to make much more than just my spring rolls: see my Sweet Summer Rolls on page 163 or the crispy snacks on page 61.

Makes 12 rolls

For the filling
1 large carrot
350g [12oz] celeriac [celery root]
2 Tbsp groundnut [peanut] oil, plus extra for deep-frying
2.5-cm [1-in] piece of root ginger, peeled and grated
1 Tbsp honey
1 Tbsp rice vinegar
2 Tbsp chopped fresh coriander [cilantro]
150g [5oz] pickled beetroot [beet]

For the wrappers
12 rice wrappers

For the sriracha mayonnaise
1 garlic clove, crushed
225g [1 cup] mayonnaise
3 Tbsp sriracha [Thai hot chilli sauce]
lemon juice

Shave the carrot into thin ribbons using a speed [swivel] peeler and then cut the ribbons into matchsticks. Peel the celeriac and cut into tiny dice. Heat 2 tablespoons of oil in a frying pan [skillet] and fry the diced celeriac and ginger over a medium-low heat until tender and golden. Drizzle over the honey, add the rice vinegar and continue to fry until the celeriac is caramelized (don't burn it!), stirring regularly. Add the coriander and set aside to cool. Finely dice the beetroot.

To assemble the spring rolls, fill a large dish with warm water, dip a rice wrapper in the water to soften it and then place it flat on a board in front of you. Spoon a little of the filling ingredients on the wrapper, one-third of the way from the edge nearest you. Roll the wrapper around the filling, folding the sides in as you go to seal the roll. Repeat with the remaining wrappers and filling to make 12 rolls.

For the sriracha mayonnaise, stir all the ingredients together. Taste and adjust, as necessary, by adding more lemon juice or sriracha.

Serve the rolls with the mayonnaise.

Peking duck salad wraps

To make Peking duck, you need a duck – fair enough. But, you also need a lifetime's experience as a Chinese chef and 5 entire days of your life. That's right. So, next time you buy one, treat it with a little more respect, which is what I'm trying to do here.

Makes 6 wraps

½ Peking duck, bought from a Chinese food store or takeaway restaurant
6 large, firm lettuce leaves, e.g. iceberg
6–12 Tbsp hoisin sauce
½ cucumber, cut into matchsticks
3 spring onions [scallions], cut into thin strips
3 chillies, thinly sliced
75g [3oz] roasted unsalted peanuts, roughly chopped
1 lime, cut into 6 wedges

Using two forks (like they do in Chinese restaurants), pull all the skin and meat off the duck, tearing it into long shreds.

Divide the duck between the lettuce leaves and spoon 1–2 tablespoons of hoisin sauce (according to how much you like) on top.

Pile on cucumber matchsticks, spring onion strips, sliced chillies and chopped peanuts and squeeze over the lime wedges. Roll the lettuce leaves around the filling, eat with your fingers – and enjoy!

4 quick snacks

Crisp-fried chickpeas

Open a can of chickpeas [garbanzo beans], drain them well and spread out in a single layer on a plate lined with kitchen paper [paper towels]. Pat the chickpeas thoroughly with more kitchen paper until they are dry. Don't peel off or discard the skins as, when the chickpeas are fried, the skins will be the crispiest part. Heat neutral flavoured oil for deep-frying to 180°C [350°F] in a deep saucepan and fry the chickpeas for 3 minutes. Take care, as to begin with the oil will spit, so stand well back from the pan. Drain the chickpeas on kitchen paper and season with salt and any spice you fancy (I'd go for cinnamon or smoked paprika).

Instant French kimchi

Mix 150g [1 cup] sauerkraut with 1 tablespoon of harissa paste. It goes without saying, you'll need to adjust the amount you add according to how much chilli you like and the strength of the harissa. When I'm not eating this with a spoon, I use it as a topping for just about anything and everything.

Nori seaweed chips

Using scissors, cut sheets of nori seaweed into strips, about a thumb-width wide and twice or three times as long. Dip a sheet of kitchen paper [paper towel] or your fingers in a neutral flavoured oil and rub over the strips (but go easy, not too much oil) and then sprinkle them with salt. Preheat the oven to 200°C/180°C fan/400°F/Gas 6. Spread out the nori strips on a baking sheet and bake for 5–10 minutes or until they start to curl up.

Fried rice wrappers

The quickest recipe ever! Heat about 1cm [½in] of neutral flavoured oil in a wok or deep frying pan. Using a pair of metal tongs, carefully lower the dry rice wrappers one at a time into the hot oil for 10 seconds or until they turn curly and crisp. Lift out, sprinkle liberally with salt and spice (how about Chinese five spice mix?).

Ahi poké salad wrap

You don't say 'ahi tuna' as 'ahi' already means yellow fin tuna in Hawaiian. The inamona relish I've made here is actually a cheat's version of genuine inamona, which is made with roasted 'Kuku' (aka known as candlenuts) and salt. Still, you've just learnt three Hawaiian words and that's pretty impressive!

Makes 2 wraps

2 Tbsp neutral flavoured oil, such as rapeseed
100g [3½oz] sashimi-grade raw tuna steak, 1cm [⅜in] thick
1 Tbsp light soy sauce
1.25-cm [½-in] piece of root ginger, grated
1 spring onion [scallion], white and green parts finely chopped and separated
1 tsp sesame seeds
1 mild chilli, deseeded and finely chopped

For the inamona relish
25g [1oz] macadamia nuts
salt (if using unsalted nuts)
1 sheet of dried nori seaweed

To serve
¼ avocado, cubed
2 large lettuce leaves
lime juice and a little grated zest
green parts of 1–2 spring onions [scallions], cut lengthwise into thin strips and left in a bowl of iced water until they curl

Heat 1 tablespoon of oil in a frying pan [skillet] over a high heat and sear the tuna steak on each side. Remove from the pan and cut the tuna into 1-cm [⅜-in] cubes. Toss in a bowl with the remaining oil to preserve its colour.

Add the soy sauce, ginger, chopped white part of the spring onion – reserving the green part for later – sesame seeds and finely chopped chilli. Cover and store in the refrigerator until needed.

For the inamona relish, roughly chop the macadamia nuts with salt (if using unsalted nuts) and the nori seaweed.

Add the green part of the spring onion to the tuna mixture, along with the cubed avocado. Stir gently until the ingredients are combined.

Spoon half the mixture onto a large lettuce leaf, squeeze over a little lime juice and sprinkle with lime zest. Fold the lettuce around the filling to enclose it. Repeat with the remaining ingredients to make 2 wraps.

Serve the wraps with the inamona and the curled green parts of the spring onions.

Reina pepiada arepa

Arepa, pronounced 'a'repa' in Spanish, are small round breads made from masarepa flour. This is a very fine flour, also known as pre-cooked white maize meal, but – a word of warning – it is different from ordinary cornflour (cornstarch), which can't be used. Arepa breads are crisp on the outside and soft and fluffy in the centre. They are a staple part of the cuisines of Colombia and Venezuela where they are eaten at any time of day – lunch, dinner or after a hard night's partying!

Makes 8

For the arepa
450ml [2 cups] tepid water
1 tsp salt
175g [1½ cups] masarepa
2 Tbsp neutral flavoured oil, plus extra for frying

For the reina pepiada filling
2 Tbsp neutral flavoured oil
2 onions, finely chopped
1 Tbsp brown sugar
450g [1lb] cooked chicken meat, shredded
2 avocados, pitted, peeled and chopped
2 garlic cloves, crushed
2 Tbsp chopped fresh coriander [cilantro]
hot chilli sauce, to taste
lime juice
salt and pepper
2–3 Tbsp mayonnaise

For the arepa, put the water and salt in a bowl, gradually sprinkle over the masarepa and stir with a spoon. Work everything together with your fingers until you have a soft, smooth-textured dough. If the dough is too sticky, add more masarepa, if it's too dry, it needs more water. Mix in the oil and then shape the dough into a ball and flatten slightly.

Cut the dough into 8 wedges. Dampen your hands to stop the dough sticking to them and roll each wedge into a ball. Flatten the balls into rounds, 2cm [¾in] thick.

Preheat the oven to 180°C/160°C fan/350°F/Gas 4.

Add a good amount of oil to a heavy frying pan [skillet] over a medium heat and fry the dough rounds for 5–10 minutes on each side until golden spots appear on them. Lift them out of the pan onto a wire rack and finish them in the oven on the rack for 10 minutes.

While the arepa are cooking, make the reina pepiada. Heat the oil in a pan and fry the onions until translucent. Sprinkle the sugar over the onions and continue to fry until caramelized but not burnt! Put the shredded chicken in a bowl, add the avocado, garlic, coriander and caramelized onions. Season with hot chilli sauce, a squeeze of lime juice, salt and pepper. Finally, stir in a bit of mayonnaise to bind everything together to make a coarse paste.

When the arepa are cooked, split them in half through the centre, just like pitta bread, and sandwich with the reina pepiada filling. Eat immediately. Thank me later.

Prawn banh mi crossed with a jambon beurre

The classic French ham sandwich, 'jambon beurre', is great but it lacks that special kick, so here I'm giving you the best of both worlds: crisp French bread filled with the lovely, tangy flavours of Vietnam.

Serves 3

For the pickled carrot
1 large carrot
vinegar (I use rice vinegar but you can use any vinegar you like)
1 Tbsp sugar
salt

For the prawn patties
6 large raw prawns [shrimp]
2 Tbsp neutral flavoured oil
drizzle of sesame oil
1 Tbsp Maggi seasoning sauce
2 garlic cloves, grated
1 tsp grated root ginger
1 egg, beaten
1 red chilli, chopped
2 Tbsp flour
pepper

To serve
1 French baguette
mayonnaise
cucumber
bean sprouts
chopped fresh coriander [cilantro]
sliced spring onions [scallions]
Maggi seasoning sauce
chopped red chilli, to garnish

To pickle the carrot, shave the carrot lengthwise into long, thin ribbons using a speed [swivel] peeler. Put the ribbons in a small bowl, pour vinegar over them, add the sugar and a little salt. Massage the carrots with your fingers so they absorb the flavour of the vinegar and sugar and then leave to infuse.

For the prawn patties, peel the prawns, reserving the heads, tails and shells. Heat the oil in a frying pan [skillet], add the heads, tails and shells and fry until they turn deep pink. Strain, discarding the prawn debris but keeping the precious prawn-infused oil.

Chop the prawns finely and put them in a mixing bowl. Add a drizzle of sesame oil, the Maggi seasoning sauce, garlic, ginger, beaten egg and chopped chilli. Stir in the flour to bind the mixture together and season with salt and pepper.

Reheat the prawn-infused oil in the frying pan and gently place tablespoons of the prawn mixture in the pan to make 6 patties – do this carefully as the oil might splash. Fry until the patties are golden brown underneath and then turn them over to brown the other side.

To assemble the prawn banh mi, cut the baguette into 3 equal lengths and cut each in half horizontally. Spread the cut sides of the bread with mayonnaise and sit 2 prawn patties on each bottom half of bread. Using a smart peeler, shave long, thin ribbons from the cucumber. Pile cucumber and drained pickled carrot ribbons on top of the patties, followed by a few bean sprouts, some chopped coriander and sliced spring onions. Finally, drizzle over a little seasoning sauce and sprinkle with chopped chilli before replacing the bread tops. I think a sandwich is best when you're struggling to close it.

Tunisian snack

Tunisia is famous for olive oil and dates but less well known for its superb canned tuna. I love cooking with food from cans as there is something very satisfying about raising the profile of simple foods as I've done here with this marvellous chilli sandwich.

Serves 3–4

1 loaf of Italian bread about 30cm
   [12in] long (see my note below)
140-g [5-oz] can of tuna in oil

For the Tunisian salad
1 large tomato
1 green [bell] pepper
½ cucumber
¼ bunch of fresh coriander [cilantro]
¼ onion
olive oil (if the oil in the can of tuna
   is good quality, I suggest you don't
   waste it but use it for dressing the
   salad)
salt and pepper
a squeeze of lemon juice

To serve
2 eggs
2 tsp harissa (personally I love it,
   so I add a bit more)
2 tsp capers
2 tsp finely chopped preserved lemons
100g [3½oz] boiled potatoes, sliced or
   chopped
1–2 chillies, chopped

Slice the bread in half lengthwise. Drain the tuna, reserving the oil, if it is good quality, for the salad.

For the Tunisian salad, chop the tomato, green pepper and cucumber into small dice. Coarsely chop three-quarters of the coriander, reserving the rest for garnishing the sandwich, and finely chop the onion. Mix everything together in a bowl with olive oil, salt, pepper and the lemon juice.

Cook the eggs for 10 minutes in a pan of boiling water. Drain and place in a bowl of cold water. When cool enough to handle, peel off the shells and slice into rounds.

Open the bread and spread the cut sides with harissa. Spoon the salad over the bottom half of the bread, followed by the tuna, broken into large flakes, the sliced eggs and, finally, the capers, preserved lemons and potatoes.

Garnish with chopped chillies and the remaining coriander leaves, replace the top half of the bread and serve.

The more you know

Italian bread has been popular in Tunisia since it was introduced there by the Italians who moved to the country for work in the 19th and early 20th centuries. Known as 'Khobz', it is a long white loaf with quite a dense texture and nigella seeds sprinkled on top. Available from north African food stores but, if you can't track it down, you could use a baguette or ciabatta instead.

12 dried spices that will make you a CHEF

I love my spices as they bring so much flavour and colour to food. They are, of course, key elements in complex curries but they can also raise a bowl of rice or pasta up to CHEF level. What is probably most important about them is that spices are not, and must never be, for the sole use of chefs! Here is a list of those I always have in my kitchen cupboard.

Black pepper – pungent and piquant

Adds depth and heat to any savoury dish but it can also be used sparingly on some desserts (for example, a touch of freshly ground black pepper is sublime on strawberries and cream).

Food pairing: pasta (definitely carbonara), steak, carrots, corn, cream, cauliflower

Chilli powder – hot and red-ish

Heat in powdered form is just too convenient not to include here. It's not commonly used in France, to my regret as heat is such an essential part of so many dishes – try to imagine Thai or Mexican food without it... see what I mean?

Food pairing: prawns [shrimp], crab, aubergine [eggplant], stir fries, beef, ramen, pork

Cinnamon – sweet and woody

Universally popular and used around the globe, particularly in Northern Europe, North America and North Africa. I use half a cinnamon stick to lightly flavour stews and marinades and the ground version to sprinkle over desserts.

Food pairing: crème brûlée, pastries, apple pies, doughnuts, Moroccan pastilla, rice (add a bay leaf and get crowned)

Cloves – powerful and menthol-y

ULTRA powerful, SUPER-pungent and MEGA menthol-y, so when it comes to size, don't trust them! Use just one (or two – how can you?) of these tiny flavour bombs to brilliantly enhance your stock but one too many will literally anaesthetize your palate forever.

Food pairing: French *pot au feu* and Vietnamese *pho bo* are the best examples

Coriander seeds – fresh and citrusy

The first spice on my list which adds freshness rather than warmth to a dish. And, hey, if you find fresh coriander [cilantro] has a soapy flavour, don't judge the seeds too quickly as they are quite different. Coriander seeds will balance the power of cumin and that's why they are often used together in dishes.

Food pairing: pickled vegetables, any curry, stews, marinades.

Cumin seeds – warm and earthy

Really powerful and used widely in Mexican, Middle Eastern, North African and Indian cuisines. I often combine them with coriander seeds as they balance each other nicely.

Food pairing: chilli, falafel, roasted parsnips, honey, parsley, black beans, onions

Fennel seeds – fresh and aniseed-y

No pepper, wood, lemon, heat or smoke here as fennel seeds bring something different – fresh aniseed. Definitely less powerful than star anise but way more versatile. Like coriander seeds it's on the fresh side but naughtier.

Food pairing: sausages (Italian), seafood, stir fries (it's part of Chinese five-spice mix)

Garlic powder – intense

I grew up in a Mediterranean environment, which meant that garlic was infused in my baby bottle (it's a joke, OK? Are you outta your mind?!). Dried garlic powder is quite intense and powerful so I usually go for garlic flakes.

Food pairing: onions, celery, carrots, ginger

Ground ginger – piquant

As with garlic, I tend to use fresh ginger whenever possible but it's always handy to have ground ginger on hand just in case.

Food pairing: use it with confidence in any marinade or Indian-inspired dish and, oh, don't forget those cakes and cookies

Nutmeg – woody and lemony

Usually sold as a whole nut to be finely grated, but beware! A little goes a long way and it can actually be toxic if you add too much. You think I'm joking? I am deadly serious.

Food pairing: savoury custards, creamy rice desserts, pie fillings, spinach... white sauces like béchamel can't really live without it

Smoked paprika – warm and deep red

I discovered this quite late in my culinary journey but immediately fell in love with its deep red colour and gentle heat but, of course, mostly with its warm vibe of a glowing fireplace.

Food pairing: pork ribs, beef brisket, fresh goat cheese, egg tortilla or any dish you want to pimp with a lil' bbq taste

Turmeric – peppery and proudly yellow

The perfect example of how important spices are in giving dishes colour! Turmeric is a vibrant visual extravaganza that you'll find everywhere in India, Pakistan and Bangladesh.

Food pairing: cauliflower, cabbage, root vegetables, rice, soups

Pizza & quiche

Magic-crust quiche Lorraine

As with pizzas or sushi, people often wrongly believe that a good quiche is judged on the quality of its filling. For me, it's the buttery flavour, the golden colour and crispy-crumbly texture of the crust that makes this iconic tart such a masterpiece. My twist – to really grab people's attention – is to add spices to the pastry.

Serves 6

For the pastry
1 tsp cumin seeds
1 tsp coriander seeds
½ tsp allspice berries
½ tsp whole black peppercorns
225g [scant 2 cups] plain [all-purpose] flour, plus extra for rolling out
115g [scant ½ cup] butter, diced and softened
½ tsp salt
1 egg
3 Tbsp milk

For the 'custard' filling
225ml [1 cup] milk
225ml [1 cup] double [heavy] cream
3 eggs
salt and pepper

150–200g [5½–7oz] best-quality smoked bacon rashers [slices]

Put a frying pan [skillet] over a high heat, add the spices and roast them for 30–60 seconds. Grind all the spices together to a fine powder and, if not using immediately, store in an airtight container.

For the pastry, in a mixing bowl, rub the flour, butter, salt and the ground spices together with your fingertips until the mixture is like fine breadcrumbs. Beat the egg with the milk and gradually work into the mixture, kneading lightly to make a smooth dough.

Preheat the oven to 200°C/180°C fan/400°F/Gas 6. Roll out the pastry on a lightly floured board until 5mm [¼in] thick and lift into a 25-cm [10-in] loose-bottomed tart tin [tart pan] that you've greased with butter and lightly floured. To stop the pastry puffing up in the centre (funny, but not practical), line it with baking parchment and weigh it down with baking beans or dried chickpeas. This technique is called 'baking blind'. Bake for 15 minutes, then remove from the oven but leave the oven on.

For the 'custard' filling, whisk the milk, cream and eggs together in a bowl and season with salt and pepper. Cut the bacon into lardons and fry them in a dry frying pan until golden.

When the pastry case comes out of the oven, remove the beans and parchment and scatter the lardons in the case. Carefully pour in the 'custard' and bake for about 45 minutes or until the filling is golden but still slightly wobbly in the centre.

NOTA BENE

It is important to knead the dough as little as possible. People often think that it's necessary to do this for a long time so it becomes smooth and elastic. This is absolutely right but only if you're making bread or pizza dough. With pastry, it's the complete opposite as you want it to be soft and crumbly...

Irregular quiche with 'shrooms and blue cheese

OK, I know that if you cut mushrooms into equal pieces they will cook evenly and if the quiche fillings are neatly arranged in the pastry case everyone will get a fair slice. But all this symmetry is boring!!! Tearing up mushrooms with your fingers creates different textures and tastes. In the same way, putting the filling ingredients randomly in the pastry case challenges you at the table as you have to decide which slice of quiche you want: would you rather have more melting cheese or more woody mushrooms? Regularity might be satisfying but irregularity stirs up emotions.

Serves 6

olive oil
300g [10½oz] wild mushrooms,
　e.g. portobello, ceps, shiitake
1 tsp butter
1 small garlic clove, crushed
2 Tbsp chopped fresh herbs, a mix
　of parsley and tarragon or thyme
salt and pepper
1 quantity of Magic-Crust Quiche
　Lorraine pastry made without
　the spices (see page 70)
100g [3½oz] soft blue cheese,
　cut into pieces
10 canned cooked whole chestnuts,
　broken into large pieces

For the 'custard' filling
225ml [1 cup] milk
225ml [1 cup] double [heavy] cream
3 eggs
salt and pepper

Heat a little oil in a frying pan [skillet] or – better still – a grill pan, over a medium-high heat and fry the mushrooms, having first taken care to either spread them flat or carefully tear them into large (about 2.5-cm [1-in]) pieces. Turn them over from time to time until they are nicely charred and then remove from the heat and set to one side.

While the mushrooms are still hot, add the butter, garlic and chopped herbs and season with salt and pepper. Stir gently and resist the urge to eat them as you'll need them later!

Preheat the oven to 200°C/180°C fan/400°F/Gas 6. Roll out the pastry on a lightly floured board until 5mm [¼in] thick and lift into a 25-cm [10-in] loose-bottomed tart tin [tart pan] that you've greased with butter and lightly floured. Bake blind for 15 minutes (see page 70). When the blind baking is done, remove from the oven but leave the oven on.

For the 'custard' filling, whisk the milk, cream and eggs together in a bowl and season with salt and pepper.

When the pastry case comes out of the oven, remove the beans and parchment and scatter the mushrooms, blue cheese and chestnuts in the case. Carefully pour in the 'custard' and bake for about 45 minutes or until the filling is golden but still slightly wobbly in the centre.

Ratatouille quiche

The word 'ratatouille' comes from the Occitan language of southern France and just means a mixed stew. But, hey, what a stew! Not only is it fresh, colourful and easy to make but it's a great way to get kids to eat their veg. Now, turn it into a quiche and – boy – those kids might become vegetarians.

Serves 6

For the ratatouille
1 large red onion
3 garlic cloves
1 red [bell] pepper
1 yellow or orange [bell] pepper
1 courgette [zucchini]
1 small aubergine [eggplant]
4 tomatoes
olive oil
1 Tbsp fresh thyme leaves

For the pastry
1 quantity of Magic-Crust Quiche
   Lorraine pastry made without
   the spices (see page 70)

For the 'custard' filling
115ml [½ cup] double [heavy] cream
115ml [½ cup] milk
3 eggs
salt and pepper

torn fresh basil leaves, to garnish

For the ratatouille, peel and cut the onion into wedges. Peel and thinly slice the garlic cloves. Deseed the peppers, trim the courgette and aubergine and cut into 2.5-cm [1-in] chunks. Quarter the tomatoes.

Heat 2–3 tablespoons of olive oil in a large casserole dish [Dutch oven] or saucepan and fry the onion and garlic over a low heat for about 5 minutes, until the onion has softened. Add the peppers, courgette, aubergine and thyme leaves, turn up the heat a little and fry for 10–15 minutes over a medium heat or until the vegetables are softened and golden, stirring from time to time. Remove the vegetables from the pan to a plate and set aside with the tomatoes.

Preheat the oven to 200°C/180°C fan/400°F/Gas 6. Roll out the pastry on a lightly floured board until 5mm [¼in] thick and lift into a 25-cm [10-in] loose-bottomed tart tin [tart pan] that you've greased with butter and lightly floured. Bake blind for 15 minutes (see page 70). When the blind baking is done, remove from the oven but leave the oven on.

For the 'custard' filling, whisk the milk, cream and eggs together in a bowl and season with salt and pepper.

When the pastry case comes out of the oven, remove the beans and parchment and spoon all the vegetables into the case, spreading them out evenly. Season with a good pinch of salt and freshly ground black pepper. Carefully pour in the 'custard', shaking the tin gently so the custard is evenly distributed.

Bake for about 30 minutes or until the filling is golden but still slightly wobbly in the centre. Serve hot with torn basil leaves scattered over.

#HACK

A crash course in making Neapolitan pizza

Except on very, very rare occasions, I don't follow recipes to the letter. I believe in free interpretation and that adding a little bit more of this or that isn't going to change the world. Except, that is, when it comes to a Neapolitan pizza. I then switch from being a relaxed and easy-going hippy to an obsessive and meticulous chemist, ready to commit murder to produce THE perfect pizza!

The dough For me, getting the pizza dough right is the key. The ingredients used are very basic – water, flour, salt and yeast – but making it is still sufficiently complex to need to learn to master it completely.

The flour Choose a wheat flour with a high protein content [<10%] and labelled 'TIPO 00', if possible. As it is ground more finely, it absorbs water better. Bread/strong flour will also do.

The yeast It doesn't matter whether it's dried or fresh; what is important is that only a very little is used [0.2% of the weight of the flour] and that rising times for the dough are sufficiently long.

Hydration Neapolitan pizza dough is well hydrated [65–70% of the weight of the flour], which makes it much more elastic and above all ensures the dough is airy and bubbly in the oven during baking.

Proving As with bread, pizza dough needs two risings: the first for 2 hours at room temperature [25°C/77°F] and then a second much longer one that I like to do in the refrigerator overnight.

Shaping A ball of dough that is well rested can be shaped quickly and without too much effort into a pizza base. Lay your hand flat on the dough and, flexing your fingers, push the air out of it towards the edges in order to form a disc, 5mm [¼in] thick in the centre and 1–2cm [⅜–¾in] thick at the outside.

Tomato sauce This is easier to make than you might think. It consists of good-quality canned San Marzano tomatoes that you simply crush with oil, salt and oregano until smooth.

Cheese Use mozzarella or *Fior di Latte*, plus Parmesan. From experience, I find a slightly dryer mozzarella releases less water and that prevents the centre from being undercooked. Avoid using too much Parmesan – it's just there to add substance.

Baking Oven cooking is essential for making a successful pizza. It must bake very quickly and at a high temperature – preheat the oven to its highest setting.

Pizza stone/steel In a traditional pizza oven, the pizza is baked from below. To replicate this at home, use a preheated pizza stone, an upturned, preheated griddle pan, or a 'baking steel', which is a stainless steel slab.

The pizza grand finale It must have a crust that's puffed and well speckled like the coat of a leopard. It must also be round and regular in shape and nicely charred on the base, with a soft centre and melted but not burnt cheese.

A confession and a transgression Basil leaves scattered on top are supposed to be baked with the pizza. That's the rule. But... I never do it. By cooking the fresh leaves you destroy their character, so I add them at the end.

Parisian pizza

When it comes to eating pizza, apparently only the USA consumes more than France and – humbly – it's probably thanks to me that we're in second place at all.

Serves 3

150g [5½oz] young asparagus spears
115g [4oz] cooked ham
75g [2¾oz] button mushrooms
75g [2¾oz] fresh goat cheese
1 Tbsp olive oil, plus extra for drizzling
salt and pepper
chopped fresh tarragon, to garnish

For super-legit pizza dough (this makes enough for 3 large pizza bases)
350ml [1½ cups] warm (not hot) water
1 Tbsp salt
525g [4 cups] flour type 00
a pinch of instant yeast

For the super-legit pizza dough, pour the water into a large bowl. Add the salt and leave until dissolved.

Whisk in 50g [scant ½ cup] of the flour, mixing well. Add the yeast and gradually mix in the rest of the flour to make a dough.

Knead the dough for about 20 minutes or until it is smooth. Cover with clingfilm [plastic wrap] and leave to rise at room temperature for 2 hours.

Portion the dough into 3 equal pieces and roll into balls. Put them in an airtight container – the container must be very wide so the dough balls don't stick together as they expand. Leave to rise at room temperature for 6 hours or, better still, for 12–36 hours in the refrigerator, as this will give the dough a better texture and flavour. Bravo! You've just made my super legit pizza dough. (If you are not using all 3 balls of dough straightaway, put the unused balls in a lightly greased bowl, cover with cling film and refrigerate for up to 2 days. Or put in sealed bags and freeze for up to 3 months; thaw in the refrigerator overnight and allow to come to room temperature before using.)

Now start your topping. Remove any tough scales from the asparagus spears, chop the ham and halve the mushrooms, leaving very tiny mushrooms whole.

Mix together the goat cheese and olive oil and season with salt and pepper.

Preheat the oven to its highest setting and, if you don't have a pizza stone, preheat an upturned griddle pan in the oven. Roll out one ball of pizza dough with a rolling pin until about 25cm [10in] in diameter. Place the pizza base on a sheet of baking parchment and spread with the goat cheese mixture. Top with the asparagus, ham and mushrooms. Drizzle with a little extra olive oil.

Slide the pizza onto the pizza stone or preheated griddle pan and bake for 5–10 minutes or until the edges of the dough are lightly charred and puffed up. Serve at once sprinkled with chopped tarragon.

Pizza marinière

The term 'marinière' usually applies to the mussels cooked in a white wine-shallot-parsley sauce that one devours greedily by the sea, eating them with your fingers, of course, and taking great care not to leave a single drop of the precious buttery juices at the bottom of the pot. Here the idea is the same but served on a pizza.

Serves 3

300g [10½oz] mussels in their shells
½ bunch of fresh flat-leaf parsley
3 medium shallots
1 tsp butter
1 tsp fresh thyme leaves
1 garlic clove, sliced
pepper
200ml [scant 1 cup] dry white wine
   or, if you don't want to use alcohol,
   substitute with 175ml [¾ cup]
   vegetable stock with a few drops
   of cider vinegar added
1 Tbsp plain [all-purpose] flour
1 Tbsp double [heavy] cream
1 ball of uncooked pizza dough
   (see page 76), ready to roll out

Clean the mussels thoroughly by rinsing under cold running water. Using a small knife, pull away the 'beards' and scrape off any barnacles. Discard any mussels with broken shells or that are already open and do not close immediately when firmly tapped.

Separate the parsley stalks and leaves. Finely chop 2 shallots and the parsley stalks. Heat the butter in a large pan with a lid over a medium heat, add the chopped shallots, thyme, garlic and chopped parsley stalks and fry uncovered until softened. Increase the heat under the pan to high, add the mussels, season with pepper and pour in the wine or stock. Cover the pan immediately and cook for 3 minutes. Take the lid off the pan, stir the mussels, put the lid back on and cook for a further 3 minutes. All the shells should have opened – discard any that remain tightly closed.

Drain the mussels from their cooking liquid and pour the liquid into a saucepan. Place the pan over a high heat and whisk in the flour until smooth. Boil until reduced by half and then add the cream. (As we're making a pizza, the sauce has to be thick.)

Preheat the oven to its highest setting and, if you don't have a pizza stone, preheat an upturned griddle pan in the oven. Roll out the ball of pizza dough with a rolling pin until about 25cm [10in] in diameter. Lay the pizza base on a sheet of baking parchment, spread the sauce over it and arrange the open mussels on top. Chop the remaining shallot and scatter over. Personally, I like to leave the mussels in their shells – it's a style thing.

Slide the pizza onto the pizza stone or preheated griddle pan and bake for 5–10 minutes or until the edges of the dough are lightly charred and puffed up. Serve at once sprinkled with chopped parsley.

Picture on page 79.

The more you know

Marinière also refers to a striped sweater worn by sailors – or hipsters – all over France. Just so you know, I've already gone sailing.

As usual this is an adaptation of a traditional recipe, my inspiration coming this time from the 'pissaladière', a savoury tart from Provence in south-east France.

Pissaladière pizza

Serves 3

3 canned sardines, drained
6 canned anchovies, drained
olive oil
3 large onions, finely chopped
salt
1 ball of uncooked pizza dough
   (see page 76), ready to roll out
1 small red [bell] pepper, deseeded
   and thinly sliced
1 small fennel bulb, thinly sliced
handful of pitted black olives
chopped thyme and rosemary
   leaves (fresh are best but
   dried are fine as well)

What to do?

If you detest anchovies, you can
   replace them with sardines,
or if that suggestion doesn't help,
replace the fish with olive tapenade.
   If you don't like olives either,
WHAT DO YOU LIKE, DAMN IT??

Blend the sardines with the anchovies. Add about 5 tablespoons of olive oil and blend again until you have a smooth paste. This is the base of our dish.

Heat 4 tablespoons of olive oil in a casserole dish or large pan with a lid, add the chopped onions and season with salt. Cover the pan and cook over a low heat for at least 1 hour. I know this sounds like hard work but you'll be able to use this onion 'compote' in all sorts of dishes. It will also keep for easily a week in the refrigerator, covered with oil, in a sealed jar.

Preheat the oven to its highest setting and, if you don't have a pizza stone, preheat an upturned griddle pan in the oven. Roll out the ball of pizza dough with a rolling pin until about 25cm [10in] in diameter. Place the pizza base on a sheet of baking parchment and spread 3 tablespoons of sardine paste over it. Beware – it's very salty and the flavour is powerful. Spread 8 tablespoons of onion compote on top and scatter over the pepper and fennel. Sprinkle over the thyme and rosemary and drizzle with olive oil.

Slide the pizza onto the pizza stone or preheated griddle pan and bake for 5–10 minutes or until the edges of the dough are lightly charred and puffed up.

Tarte flambée pizza

Tarte flambée is a speciality of Alsace in eastern France, where it's also known as flammekueche. To me it's every inch a pizza; in shape, in how it's made and how it's cooked. The pastry was the only thing I had a problem with as I found it a bit dry and less flavoursome than those wonderful crusts from Naples. Well, problem solved. As you can tell, it's exactly the same.

Serves 3

50g [2oz] good-quality smoked bacon rashers [slices] – don't stint on these
a little olive oil
1 small onion. chopped
100g [scant ½ cup] ricotta or full-fat natural Greek yogurt
4 Tbsp thick crème fraîche, 30% fat
salt and pepper
freshly grated nutmeg
1 ball of uncooked pizza dough (see page 76), ready to roll out

Cut the bacon into small lardons.

Heat a little olive oil in a frying pan [skillet] and fry the bacon and onions over a very low heat until the onions are translucent.

In a bowl, mix together the ricotta or yogurt and crème fraîche. Season with salt and pepper and a little grated nutmeg.

Preheat the oven to its highest setting and, if you don't have a pizza stone, preheat an upturned griddle pan in the oven. Roll out one ball of pizza dough with a rolling pin until about 20–25cm [8–10in] in diameter. Place the round of pizza dough on a sheet of baking parchment and spread the cream mixture over it. Top with the onions and bacon lardons.

Slide the pizza onto the pizza stone or preheated griddle pan and bake for 5–10 minutes or until the edges of the dough are lightly charred and puffed up.

DON'T PANIC

Making pizza dough needs a bit of time to master. You'll find the recipe on page 76, with plenty of helpful tips on the preceding page, but if your courage fails you, ready-made dough bought from a supermarket will do the job. And don't be too hard on yourself as we don't always have time to make everything from scratch.

Carbs

Comté cacio e pepe pasta

Comfort food Italian style, except I've made it French. Spaghetti, pici, tonarelli, linguine... you could use almost any type of pasta for this recipe but go for round shapes rather than flat ones. The challenge is to transform a hard and dry cheese into a silky, smooth sauce – which I'm here to show you how to do.

Serves 4

300g [10½oz] pasta of your choice
150g [1½ cups] grated Comté cheese at room temperature, plus a little extra to serve
freshly ground or cracked black pepper

GOOD TO KNOW

I've used the French cheese Comté for this recipe. You can find it pretty much everywhere but if you have trouble tracking it down or you're feeling frugal (in French, when you don't want to spend much money, we say 'if you have sea urchins in your pockets' – ouch!), you can of course use any hard cheese (such as Parmesan, Grana Padano, Pecorino...)

Cook the pasta in a wide, deep pan, as you would for making a risotto. You want just enough salted water in the pan to cover the pasta. Using just a little water increases the amount of starch it contains from the pasta, which will make producing a smooth sauce easier later.

After 5 minutes of cooking the pasta, transfer 225ml [1 cup] of the cooking water to a separate bowl and replace it in the pan with fresh boiling water. Finish cooking the pasta according to the instructions on the packet.

Put the grated cheese and 4 grinds of black pepper in a large dish and very slowly beat in the water drained from the pasta, as though you wanted to make a mayonnaise. The idea is to achieve a syrupy sauce.

Add the drained pasta and mix well, making sure every piece of pasta is coated in sauce. Add a little more of the cooking water from the pasta if necessary.

Serve at once with a little more cheese sprinkled over each serving and a final grind of the pepper mill.

Seafood butter – fold 1 sheet of nori seaweed several times over itself and, using scissors, cut into very fine confetti. Work into salted butter and enjoy.

Spiced butter – a good pinch of chilli flakes mixed into a little salted butter will make hairs grow on the chest of any dish. The idea sounds a bit weird but the butter is deadly.

Miso butter – mix unsalted butter and miso paste (it doesn't matter which colour) together in a ratio of 2:1 butter to miso.

Garlic and parsley butter – grate a small garlic clove, finely chop 6 leaves of flat-leaf parsley and combine them with a large knob of salted butter. It's very French 'old school' but, gee, it's good...

Potato gnocchi with butter

This recipe came about because I don't always have potatoes at home but I do have a packet of instant potato flakes – they're super for making mash for my son and his fantastic dad (me!). I've included 4 tasty butters to up the gnocchi's 'wow' factor.

Serves 4

125g [1 cup] plain [all-purpose] flour, plus extra for rolling out
200g [2 cups] instant potato flakes
1 egg, beaten
225ml [1 cup] water
½ tsp fine sea [kosher] salt
salted butter or one of the flavoured butters opposite, to serve

Put the flour and potato flakes in a large bowl and stir to mix. Make a well in the centre and pour in the egg and water and add the salt. Stir everything together to make a soft, smooth dough, dust the worktop lightly with flour and roll the dough into long cylinders, about 2cm [¾in] in diameter with your hands. Cut into roughly 2-cm [¾-in] lengths with a knife. We call these 'small pillows' in French – yes, really.

Cook the dough pieces in a saucepan of boiling water for about 2 minutes – when they float they are ready. Drain and serve hot tossed with salted or flavoured butter. These gnocchi are one of the most comforting dishes I know. You can even serve them cold without butter and they're still pretty good to eat.

French fries and poutine

Now here's a confession: French fries aren't French. They actually come from Belgium and I have to say the Belgians are extremely good at making them. Crispy on the outside, fluffy on the inside, and beautifully golden, they're absolutely nothing like the limp, barely-cooked sticks you find all the time in fast food places.

Serves 4

1kg [2lb 4oz] large potatoes, e.g. Maris Piper, Sebago, Bintje, Russet
groundnut [peanut] oil for deep-frying
3 Tbsp butter
3 Tbsp plain [all-purpose] flour
about 350ml [1½ cups] dark beef stock
salt
60g [about ½ cup] white Cheddar cheese curds or chunks of semi-dry mozzarella

Another confession

La poutine is a Canadian dish from Quebec so, as far as I can see, there's nothing very French about this recipe...

Peel the potatoes and cut them into sticks, 1cm [½in] thick. If they're too thin, they'll overcook when you fry them and if they're too thick, they'll be raw in the centre... Just saying.

Pour the oil into a large, heavy-based saucepan or deep-fryer – but don't fill the pan more than half-full – and heat the oil to 130°C [270°F]. It's important to use a cooking thermometer and to check it regularly to make sure the oil is at just the right temperature.

Fry the potatoes in batches for 7–10 minutes or until they are tender when pierced with a skewer or the tip of a knife but they haven't started to colour. Drain each batch onto a plate lined with kitchen paper [paper towels] before you add the next to the pan.

Heat the butter in a saucepan over a medium heat. When melted, take the pan off the heat and stir in the flour until smooth and then cook until the mixture becomes caramel-coloured. Gradually stir in the stock and bring to the boil, stirring constantly until smooth and syrupy – the amount of stock you add will depend on how thick you want your sauce to be. Instant gravy – done.

Keep the gravy warm over a low heat while you finish frying the chips. Reheat the oil to a higher temperature this time – 180°C [350°F] – to ensure the fries are really crisp. Fry all the potatoes in one go until they are done to your liking – personally I prefer them brown rather than golden so in my case I'd do this for 4 minutes but you might prefer yours golden, so reduce the frying time a bit. Drain as above and immediately sprinkle the fries generously with salt.

Divide the fries between serving bowls, scatter over the cheese and spoon over the hot gravy.

Jewelled Persian rice

This recipe might have been called; 'How to finally master the art of cooking basmati rice, make it really colourful and pretty with saffron, and add different sweet and savoury textures'. I then said to myself 'maybe that's a bit long for a title' but it does tell you everything you need to know.

Serves 4

350g [1¾ cups] of the best
   basmati rice you can buy
12 saffron threads
1 large orange
50g [2oz] shelled unsalted pistachios
2 Tbsp dried barberries
   (or chopped sour cherries)

A CONFESSION

Although this recipe might dazzle with its rich colours and textures, it happens that some evenings I have nothing to add to my bowl of rice. So, what do I do then? Well, I just enjoy the gentle heat coming from the bowl, the natural beauty of the long grains of rice, each one beautifully separate, and the delicate perfume of butter that I've gently heated until it melts before drizzling over the rice.

Put the rice in a large bowl and pour over enough cold water to cover. Stir with your hand and when the water becomes cloudy, replace it with fresh. Repeat this process at least 3 times. "Why?", you ask. Well, it's a fair question. The reason is that by soaking and rinsing the rice, you get rid of the natural starch it contains that makes the grains stick together as they cook. So – OK – when you're making a risotto, you don't rinse the rice. Get it?

Cover the rice with fresh water one last time and let it soak for 20 minutes. Drain in a colander and run cold water through to rinse it. Tip the rice into a saucepan and add 900ml [3¾ cups] cold water.

Crush the saffron threads and place in a small, heatproof jar. Add 2 tablespoons of boiling water and screw the lid on the jar.

Bring the rice to the boil, lower the heat, put a lid on the pan and stand the warm, sealed jar on top. Leave the jar there while simmering the rice for 10–12 minutes. Now remove the jar, leave the lid on the pan and let the rice sit for 5 minutes. Finally, lightly fork through the grains to fluff them up.

Transfer half the cooked rice to a bowl and pour in the infused saffron. Stir gently with a fork until the liquid from the saffron has been absorbed by the rice.

Using a speed [swivel] peeler, shave the zest from the orange in wide ribbons and then cut these into very fine strips. Chop the pistachios.

Spoon the white rice and yellow rice into a shallow dish and add half the strips of orange zest, half the pistachios and half the barberries. Stir gently to mix everything together, but without crushing the rice grains, and scatter over the remaining orange zest, pistachios and barberries.

Gratin dauphinois

A dish from my childhood that brings back all kinds of happy memories and reminds me of the comfort and warmth of home. My mother would prepare the gratin in a large oval dish and, ever since, I've always made mine in a large oval dish as well - but a red one. I have an awful lot of trouble understanding why people persist in preparing their gratin in a rectangular dish and, even worse, one that's blue.

Serves 6–8

about 10 medium-sized, firm-fleshed, waxy potatoes (don't use floury ones), total weight about 1.5kg [3lb 5oz], peeled
salt and pepper
450ml [2 cups] whole milk
450ml [2 cups] double [heavy] cream
1 bay leaf
pinch of freshly grated nutmeg
40g [about ⅓ cup] grated cheese, e.g. Parmesan, Cheddar, Comté (strictly speaking, the cheese is optional... But is it really?)

Cut the potatoes into 5-mm [¼-in] thick slices. Don't wash them as it's their starch that is going to thicken the sauce. Season the slices with salt and pepper.

Put the potatoes in a saucepan, add the milk, cream and bay leaf and simmer gently for about 10 minutes. Lift out the potatoes with a slotted spoon into a bowl and set them aside. Season the milk and cream with the nutmeg and, if necessary, salt and pepper. Discard the bay leaf.

Preheat the oven to 180°C/160°C fan/350°F/Gas 4.

Layer the potato slices and cream mixture alternately in a greased ovenproof dish, seasoning lightly between the layers.

Bake in the oven for 40–45 minutes or until the potatoes are tender when pierced with a skewer or the tip of a knife. Take the dish out of the oven and switch on the grill [broiler]. Sprinkle over the grated cheese and grill until the top is golden and crusty.

VEGAN ALTERNATIVE

By replacing the cream with coconut cream and the milk with almond milk, plus 1 teaspoon of cornflour (cornstarch) - but following pretty much the same steps - you get a decent dairy-free alternative that's not just fine for vegans but is also lighter. There are plenty of vegan cheeses to choose from for the crispy topping.

Make the gratin 24 hours ahead
and reheat when you want to
serve it as it will be even better.
This is due to a complex alchemy
developing between the potatoes
and the cream, which changes the
structure of the gratin, making it
firmer and the layers more even.

Macaroni cheese gratin

This is my version of an American classic but, of course, I've given it a French twist. I know a traditional mac'n'cheese must be rich and creamy all the way through but this one has a crusty topping. Sigh. I admit I'm breaking all the rules but as it's not the only time I'll be doing that in this book, I don't feel too bad about it.

Serves 6

400g [3½ cups] elbow macaroni
3 Tbsp salted butter
3 Tbsp plain [all-purpose] flour
450ml [2 cups] cold whole milk
1 egg yolk
400g [4 packed cups] grated
    cheese, e.g. Cheddar, Emmental,
    Fontina, Colby
salt and pepper
pinch of grated nutmeg
    (OK, I know I've lost it)
mushrooms, optional
    (thank goodness for that)
pinch of thyme (are you kidding?)

Cook the macaroni in a saucepan of boiling, salted water for at least 2 minutes less than the time indicated on the packet. Drain and set aside.

Add the butter and flour to the saucepan. Stir for a few minutes over a medium heat with a spatula until you have a smooth paste, but without letting the mixture colour.

Add the milk, a little at a time, stirring constantly until the sauce comes to the boil and is thickened and smooth. Take the pan off the heat, mix the egg yolk with a little of the sauce and stir this back into the rest of the sauce in the pan. Add three-quarters of the grated cheese, mix it in and then season with salt, pepper and nutmeg.

Give yourself a pat on the back as you have just made a genuine fancy-schmancy French classic called Mornay Sauce – so how about that?

Preheat the oven to 200°C/180°C fan/400°F/Gas 6. Cut the mushrooms into small pieces, if using.

Mix together the slightly under-cooked macaroni, the sauce, thyme and mushrooms and spoon into a large gratin dish. Sprinkle over the rest of the grated cheese and bake in the oven for 20 minutes until crispy on top and melting and creamy underneath.

The weekly Chinese fried rice

I make this recipe, or a variation of it, at least once a week. I vary it according to what I have to hand in the fridge but the method is always more or less the same. So here it is...

Serves 2

For an instant sauce
1 tsp soy sauce
1 tsp water
a few drops of Shaoxing wine
a few drops of sesame oil

For the fried rice
2 Tbsp neutral flavoured oil
1 egg, beaten
2 bacon rashers [slices], cut into lardons
75g [½ cup] raw prawns [shrimp], chopped
2-cm [¾-in] piece of root ginger, peeled and grated
1 garlic clove, crushed
125g [1 cup] cooked long-grain rice
3 Tbsp peas or chopped courgettes [zucchini] or celery (or any cooked green veg, chopped or sliced, if necessary)

To serve
1 spring onion [scallion], finely chopped
a pinch of chilli flakes

Make the sauce by mixing all the ingredients together.

For the fried rice, heat 1 tablespoon of the oil in a large frying pan [skillet] or wok over a very high heat. Before the pan becomes too hot, pour the beaten egg into it and stir until scrambled and just set. Scrape the egg out of the pan onto a plate and set aside. Add the remaining oil to the pan and briefly stir-fry the bacon and prawns. Before the bacon starts to brown, add the ginger and garlic, followed by the rice, and stir-fry briskly for 2 minutes.

Add the peas (or whichever green veg you're using), the scrambled egg and the sauce. Stir-fry for 1 minute or until everything is piping hot. Divide between 2 plates or bowls and serve at once sprinkled with the chopped spring onion and a dusting of chilli flakes.

Talking about rice...

Leftover rice from the night before is always a bit dry, which is normally a pain but here it's a plus. Let me explain. The enemy of caramelization is water so rice that is a little dry will caramelize and become crisp more quickly than rice that is freshly cooked and therefore still full of water. This recipe is a great way to use up leftover rice, but to avoid a potentially nasty bout of food poisoning, put it in the fridge as soon as it's cool; if the rice is left sitting around at room temperature, any bacteria it contains will begin to grow and multiply. Use the rice the next day and make sure it's piping hot and steaming before you serve it.

6 French cheeses and 21 alternatives from around the world

A cheese board really is the most satisfying experience you can possibly share on special occasions with your friends and family. Here is a selection of six very different but equally iconic French cheeses... BUT WAIT! Since I know that most of you won't have easy access to them, I'm also giving you some alternatives from around the world.

Comté

Strength: 2 out of 5
Stinky-ness: 1 out of 5

Smooth and semi-hard, sometimes crumbly. A pressed and cooked cheese made from cow milk that is produced in eastern France in the Jura mountains. Comté is aged for at least 4 months but more likely for about 8 months (the bigger the rind, the more mature the cheese). It has mild, milky, caramelized and toasted aromas with a hint of spice like nutmeg.

World alternatives Swiss Gruyère; young British Cheddar; Wisconsin Pleasant Ridge Reserve; Vermont Tarentaise

Roquefort (you don't pronounce the 't')

Strength: 5 out of 5
Stinky-ness: 4 out of 5

Sharp and buttery flavour. An unpressed and uncooked crumbly cheese made from full-fat sheep milk in south-west France or, more precisely, the Aveyron region. It belongs to the blue cheese family, is marbled throughout with blue-ish penicillium veins, which give it a distinct, pungent smell.

World alternatives Italian Gorgonzola; British Blue Stilton; Danish Blue; or even Iowa Blue Maytag

MYTH BUSTER – does cheese really stink?

When smelling a cheese, most of us fight the sensations coming from our nose, which inevitably makes the mind shut down and prevents the experience being enjoyable! The truth is cheese doesn't really stink; it just smells strong. So, the answer to my question is 'no'. (Unless, of course, we're talking Epoisses, in which case YES, cheese definitely does stink! Does that make sense?)

Ossau-Iraty

Strength: 2 out of 5
Stinky-ness: 2 out of 5

Semi-hard, smooth and mild. A pressed and uncooked cheese made from sheep milk from the Pyrenees in south-west France. As soon as you unwrap it, you immediately get the funky sheep vibe but generally it smells quite fresh and nutty.

World alternatives Spanish Manchego; young Italian Pecorino; US Gran Queso from Wisconsin

Crottin

Strength: 3 out of 5
Stinky-ness: 3 out of 5

Small soft-ripened cheese made from goat milk. The rind is quite thin but covered with an intricate pattern of wrinkles, making it beautiful, like a maze. Inside, it's whiter and usually has two distinct textures – creamy and chalky.

World alternatives Italian Robiola di Capra; Bonne Bouche from Vermont; Californian Humboldt Fog

Epoisses

Strength: 2 out of 5
Stinky-ness: 5 out of 5

Brick coloured with a soft and creamy texture. A washed-rind cheese (they use brandy liquor) made from cow milk in Burgundy in central France. Its flavour is the direct opposite of its smell, as inside it's rich and velvety.

World alternatives Irish Ardrahan; German Limburger; British Stinking Bishop; Italian Taleggio

Brie

Strength: 2 out of 5
Stinky-ness: 2 out of 5

A smooth soft-ripened cheese made from cow milk with a fluffy, white, marbled rind. The inside can vary from crumbly to creamy, depending on its age. It has the aroma of fresh mushrooms but closer to cultivated than foraged fungi.

World alternatives Since Brie is produced all over the world, tracking it down won't be a problem. To name but a few: King Island Dairy Brie from Australia; Cornish Brie from the UK; any Brie made in the US.

Pancakes

French crêpes: you can do this

Crêpes in France are much larger and thinner than those in the UK or USA but there's no need to feel intimidated about making them. The secret is the batter, which is runnier and thinner in France, as double the quantity of milk is added. This makes the batter spread out more quickly to the edges of the pan. Feeling better now?

Makes 12–18 crêpes

about 450ml [scant 2 cups] whole milk
3 eggs
125g [1 cup] plain [all-purpose] flour
a large pinch of sugar
a pinch of salt
3 Tbsp butter

In a large bowl, whisk together 350ml [1½ cups] of the milk and the eggs. Gradually add the flour, whisking all the time, so the batter thickens slowly without any lumps forming. I find this way of making the batter efficient but terribly slow. If you have a blender or food mixer, chuck everything in it, blitz or whizz together and that's it. The texture of the batter should be close to that of buttermilk, so if it's too thick, add more milk, a little at a time. Finally, whisk in the sugar and salt.

Have a large (larger than your frying pan [skillet]) heatproof bowl of cold water to hand. Put your largest frying pan over a medium-high heat and add the butter. It will melt, become mousse-like and then start to 'sing' more and more loudly. When it begins to settle down – and particularly before it becomes too amber-coloured – take the pan off the heat and dip the base in the bowl of cold water to stop the butter cooking any more. Carefully pour this 'noisette' butter into the batter, stirring all the time.

Wipe out the pan with kitchen paper [paper towels] and put it back on the heat. The technique for cooking crêpes isn't complicated but it demands a certain amount of organization. So, have the bowl of batter with a ladle in it beside the hob, the frying pan in front of you, a sheet of oiled kitchen paper within reach and finally a large plate with a lid to cover it on the other side.

Lift the pan with your right hand (I'm right-handed) and pour a ladle of batter into it. At the same time as you pour, swirl and tilt the pan in all directions. The entire base of the pan must be covered with the batter.

When the crêpe has almost finished producing steam – after about 1–2 minutes – release it from the pan with a spatula and flip it over. Continue cooking until both sides of the crêpe are evenly golden brown. Slide the crêpe out of the pan onto the plate and keep it covered while you cook the rest of the batter, rubbing the pan between each crêpe with the oiled kitchen paper.

SWEET OR SAVOURY?

In France and the UK, the tradition is to eat sweet crêpes with either butter and sugar or sugar and lemon. However, after having tasted a crêpe with ham, cheese and spring onions, you'll realize that this convention is so last year.

Goat cheese,
baby spinach
and walnuts

Aubergine, roasted
tomatoes and
toasted pine nuts

Banana, pecans and maple syrup

Red berries, almonds and cream

4 sweet toppings for crêpes

Even though a crêpe with sugar and butter is still my favourite, by adding a few toppings without reheating the crêpe, you can transform this little treat into a grand dessert. It works brilliantly.

Banana, pecans and maple syrup

1 banana, 5 pecan halves, 1 Tbsp maple syrup, finely grated zest of ½ lime

Cut the banana into thin slices. Break the pecans into small pieces. Put these on a crêpe, drizzle over the maple syrup and scatter with the lime zest. The zest will counterbalance the sweetness perfectly.

Yogurt, honey and pistachios

3 Tbsp full-fat natural Greek yogurt, 1 Tbsp runny [clear] honey, 5–10 roasted and salted pistachios, chopped into small pieces

Lightly mix the yogurt, honey and half the pistachios together and spread over the crêpe. Scatter the rest of the pistachios over the filled and folded crêpe.

Red berries, almonds and cream

5–10 red berries (strawberries, raspberries, blackcurrants and/or redcurrants), 2 Tbsp double [heavy] cream, a few flaked [slivered] almonds

Roughly crush the red berries without reducing them to a pulp. Lightly fold them into the cream. Toast the flaked almonds as this will boost their flavour. Spoon onto a crêpe.

If you've got some basil, scatter over a few small leaves just before serving so you can play the part of the great chef.

Hazelnuts and chocolate

5–10 hazelnuts, 1 Tbsp dark [semisweet] chocolate, melted, 1 Tbsp sweetened condensed milk

Chop the hazelnuts into small pieces. Heat the chocolate in the microwave and mix with the condensed milk. Spoon onto a crêpe and scatter over the hazelnuts.

Picture on pages 102–103.

Buckwheat crêpes: you can do this, too

I said to myself that if I gave this recipe a straightforward title instead of its French name (galette), you'd panic less and that would reduce the chance of you depriving yourself of a dish whose taste changed my perception of things. Whereas the taste of wheat is light, sweet and buttery, that of buckwheat is mysterious, toasty and nutty, and above all, it has a long aftertaste.

Makes about 8 crêpes

125g [1 cup] buckwheat flour
350ml [1½ cups] water (add an extra 60ml [¼ cup] if you skip the beer)
60ml [¼ cup] brown ale (if it's alcohol-free you'll need a little more water)
1 egg
a big pinch of salt
oil for the pan
a bit of butter

Mix all the ingredients together in a large bowl until you have a smooth, silky batter. It's optional, but if you let the batter rest overnight in the refrigerator, its flavour will be more pronounced.

Put a large, flat-bottomed frying pan [skillet] over a high heat and let it heat up a bit. Dip a piece of kitchen paper [paper towel] in oil and rub it over the inside of the pan.

Lift up the pan with one hand and, with the other, pour in a ladleful of batter. It's important that when the batter goes into the pan you hear a good sizzling sound. Swirl and tip the pan so the batter covers the base in a thin, even layer. To start with you'll most likely find it difficult to produce a neat, even circular shape but in time you'll get the hang of it.

When the crêpe colours underneath and gives off less steam, it's time to turn it over with a spatula. Rub the cooked side with butter and cook the other side until the crêpe is done.

It's the texture that determines the success of the finished dish. The crêpe should be brown and satin-like, dotted with hundreds of little holes, lightly crisp on the outside and melt-in-the-mouth in the middle.

SIMPLY THE BEST

My favourite crêpe is served plain with no toppings. Rien. Nada. Just the buckwheat, the Maillard reaction (the browning process), the butter and me. They are the dream team (and also the best way of determining if the crêpe is good.)

4 savoury toppings for buckwheat crêpes

There are an infinite number of toppings that you can pile onto a buckwheat crêpe. However, three are enough to produce a balanced dish: a star with a stand-out personality, a second player in a reliable supporting role, and finally a challenger to spice up the action. Take a crêpe, reheat it for 1 minute in a frying pan and top with one of the following combinations.

Scallops flambéed in whisky, with cream and leeks

2 scallops, oil for frying, a shot of whisky, 1 Tbsp double [heavy] cream, ½ small leek

Slice the scallops in half horizontally (if they are thinner they will fit more easily into the crêpe), brush lightly with oil and season well. Sear them in a frying pan [skillet] over a very high heat.

Take the pan off the heat, pour in the whisky and set alight, taking great care to avoid the flame that might shoot up! (Clue: don't lean forward with your head over the pan to check when it is going to go out...). Add the cream and set to one side.

Slice the leek into thin rounds and fry in a little oil in a frying pan until they are nicely browned. Spoon the filling onto a warm crêpe and fold up to serve.

Sausage, potato and wholegrain mustard

1–2 potatoes, oil for frying, 1 sausage, 1 Tbsp wholegrain mustard

Cut the potatoes into thin slices, 2–3mm [⅛in] thick, season and toss them in a little oil. Cook in a frying pan [skillet] until they are nicely browned. Remove from the pan and keep warm while you fry the sausage.

Add the sausage to the pan and fry until browned and cooked all the way through. Take the pan off the heat and cut the sausage into slices. Save the juices from the pan and mix them with the mustard. Spoon the filling onto a warm crêpe and fold up to serve.

Goat cheese, baby spinach and walnuts

40g [1½oz] firm goat cheese, 2 handfuls of baby spinach leaves, 5 walnut halves

This is the quickest to make. Cut the goat cheese into slices, 5mm [¼in] thick. Wash and dry the spinach leaves. Break the walnut halves into small pieces. Spoon the filling onto a warm crêpe and fold up to serve.

Aubergine, roasted tomatoes and toasted pine nuts

½ aubergine [eggplant], oil for frying, sea salt, 2–3 roasted tomatoes in a jar, 2 tsp pine nuts

Cut the aubergine into thick slices and fry over a gentle heat in a little olive oil and salt. After 20–30 minutes, they will be soft inside and caramelized on the outside.

Drain the roasted tomatoes and cut them into small pieces. Optional: you can toast the pine nuts in a dry frying pan to give them a better colour. Spoon the filling onto a warm crêpe and fold up to serve.

Picture on pages 102–103.

My go-to buttermilk pancakes

There are times in life to be bold, adventurous and even a little bit crazy. And then... there are times for having a hot breakfast under the duvet, eating comfort food that has nothing to prove. My go-to pancake recipe is exactly that. Something you already know you'll love and that will make you feel good. Phew.

Makes 16–20 pancakes

250g [2 cups] plain [all-purpose] flour
2 tsp baking powder
1 tsp salt
2 Tbsp sugar
2 eggs
350ml [1½ cups] buttermilk
4 Tbsp melted, cooled butter,
   plus extra for greasing

Serving suggestions
maple syrup
crisp-fried bacon or fresh berries

Sift the flour, baking powder and salt into a mixing bowl and stir in the sugar.

Whisk the eggs and buttermilk together in another bowl or large jug until mixed and then very gradually whisk in the melted butter. Add to the dry ingredients, stirring lightly until everything is just combined – don't beat vigorously until the batter is smooth, as it should be lumpy.

Heat a large, heavy-based non-stick frying pan [skillet] and grease lightly by rubbing a little melted butter [or oil] over it. Spoon 2 or 3 tablespoons of the batter into the pan for each pancake (cook 3 or 4 pancakes at a time) and cook for 2 minutes until the pancakes are golden brown underneath and bubbles appear on top. Flip the pancakes over and cook for another 2 minutes or until they are golden brown on the other side.

Remove from the pan and keep the pancakes warm in a clean tea towel while you cook the rest of the batter.

Serve warm topped with maple syrup and crisp-fried bacon or fresh berries.

TIP

Go easy with the stirring when you make the batter as it absolutely must not be over-mixed. If you beat it until it's smooth, you'll get the gluten in the flour working too hard and end up with tough, chewy pancakes. Yuck.

Buttermilk pancakes made with different grains

Why on earth make your pancakes just with wheat flour when there are dozens of different grains in this world? Here I'm giving you four but, remember, step out of your comfort zone and the world is your oyster!

Chickpea pancakes
Makes about 12 pancakes

Drain a 400-g [14-oz] can of chickpeas [garbanzo beans] and rinse them well. Tip the chickpeas into a blender, add 1 egg and blend a little bit. Add 115ml [½ cup] buttermilk, 1 tsp baking powder, a drizzle of oil, 1 Tbsp sugar and ½ tsp salt and blitz everything together until smooth. Using kitchen paper [paper towels], rub a frying pan [skillet] with a little oil and place it over a medium heat. Cook the pancakes in the same way as for my go-to buttermilk pancakes (page 107) – they'll just take a bit longer. Other than that, they're perfect!

Rye pancakes
Makes about 16 pancakes

Mix together 60g [½ cup] rye flour with 60g [½ cup] plain [all-purpose] flour, 1 tsp baking powder, ½ tsp salt and 2 Tbsp sugar. Measure 350ml [1½ cups] buttermilk into a jug and whisk half into the dry ingredients. Beat 1 egg and the remaining buttermilk together and whisk into the flour mixture until just combined (lumps are fine). Grease a frying pan [skillet] with a little oil and cook the pancakes over a medium heat as before.

Polenta pancakes
Makes about 12 pancakes

Mix together 80g [⅔ cup] plain [all-purpose] flour, 50g [⅓ cup] instant polenta [yellow cornmeal], 1 Tbsp sugar, 1 tsp baking powder and ½ tsp salt. Whisk 1 egg with 150ml [⅔ cup] buttermilk and 4 Tbsp neutral flavoured oil and stir into the dry ingredients until lightly mixed. Grease a frying pan [skillet] with a little oil and cook the pancakes over a medium heat as before.

Buckwheat pancakes
Makes about 14 pancakes

Mix together 140g [1 cup] buckwheat flour, 2 Tbsp sugar, 2 tsp baking powder and ½ tsp salt. In another bowl or jug, whisk together 2 Tbsp melted butter, 300ml [1¼ cups] buttermilk and 1 egg. Add the milk mixture to the dry ingredients and stir until just combined – again, the mixture should be lumpy. Grease a frying pan [skillet] with a little oil and cook the pancakes over a medium heat as before.

#HACK

How to fool everyone into thinking you're a French chef

In this book, I've tried to get rid of the snobby elitism sometimes typical of French haute cuisine. Here it's the opposite, as my aim is to make you appear to your friends like a Michelin-starred Parisian chef but at a fraction of the cost. I confess there is also the sadistic pleasure of being surprised when others don't know the 'really, really, common' French term you've just used.

Au bain marie

[say: oh-bahn-mah-ree]
This is nothing more than a double boiler but, I agree, it does sound much posher. Here's what you say:

'Of course, you can't make a sabayon (another one!) in a pan directly over the heat, it has to be cooked *au bain marie*. Gosh.'

Beurre maître d'hôtel

[say: buhr-meh-tru-doh-tell]
If you mash butter with crushed garlic and chopped parsley, you'll get a beauty that will melt seductively over steak, chicken breast or even fish. The conversation goes like this:

'Last night I made her my famous *entrecote maître d'hôtel* [the 'with *beurre*' is silent].'
'What did she say?'
'Man, she was practically weeping with joy!'

Bisque

[say: bee-ss-kuh]
Any fish or shellfish soup can be called a *bisque* if it's been thickened with a bit of butter and flour mashed together (that's a *beurre manié* by the way). Probably one of the snobbiest big guns in your French arsenal.

'In my opinion, making a soup was a mistake but I guess a *bisque* was too much to ask...'

Bouquet garni

[say: boo-keh-gahr-nee]
Using thin string, tie together several sprigs of parsley and thyme, a celery stalk and a bay leaf. This aromatic bundle is used like a teabag to flavour soups, stocks and sauces. As in:

'When he/she slowly wrapped his/her arms around me, I felt like a *bouquet garni*.'

Consommé

[say: konh-soa-meh]
This is just a clear broth or stock but I reckon it sounds posh, even to me. I love it and I can't wait to slip it into the conversation when I next see my friends at a party – haha.

Jus

[say: jüüh]
I can honestly say I'd use this one to show off as well. A *jus* is a stock or sauce that has been well reduced so it's packed with bold flavours.

'Yes, the food was great but, for God's sake, he needs to put a little more love into his *jus*!!!'

And – just so you know – it can also mean coffee.

Meat & fish

Chef vs street – how do you chop an onion?

One of the first techniques that I mastered in the kitchen was how to chop an onion. As the onion is economical, full of flavour and present in every recipe on the planet, I'd advise you to do the same.

From a very serious and very French manual, I learned the classic way of chopping an onion according to the rule book and, indeed, it works very well.

But one day, watching a video on YouTube, I learned another method used by streetfood sellers in India. I felt as though I'd received a slap in the face. This method is certainly less precise but much quicker (although, until you've got the hang of it, take it easy and watch your fingers).

I love it when everyday cooking gets one over on chef cuisine. It makes me happy. Here are the two techniques for you to decide which one suits you best.

The traditional method

For this technique, you will need any chef's knife or paring knife.

Cut the onion in half, remove the skin and lay one half, cut side down, so it is flat with the root away from you.

Make vertical cuts down the onion half. This is when you determine how thick your chopped pieces will be.

Make two horizontal cuts across it (sounds daft to me but, as they mention it, I've added it here).

Turn the half onion 90 degrees so the root is on the left (I'm a rightie).

Chop it, with your fingers tucked under (like a claw) so they are away from the knife blade.

When the half becomes unstable (too tall and with a narrow base), flip it on its side and continue chopping until only the root itself remains. Repeat with the other onion half.

The streetfood method

For this technique, you will need a very sharp knife with a long, straight, thin blade.

Slice off a big piece at the top of the onion and a smaller piece at the base. Remove the skin. The onion must be able to stand upright on its root.

Run the knife blade down top to bottom through one half of the onion to make 4 or 5 vertical slashes but without going as far as the root. The idea is to use the length of the knife so that the tip stops as it touches the chopping board.

Spin the onion 90 degrees and do the same again on the other side.

The onion is still upright but is now scored into small dice. Let it fall on its side so it flattens out a bit and chop the rest.

When you reach the root, lie it flat and chop that as well.

This method requires more practice to perfect but when you have kilos of onions to chop, it is devilishly efficient.

A perfectly cooked steak

Be warned: my way of cooking steak is a bit of a pain. Having said that, the end result is beyond epic. It involves using state-of-the-art culinary techniques like sous-vide and temperature control... But, don't panic. It's me and I promise I'll keep it cheap, fun and easy. Let's do it!

Everyone knows how they like their steak but fewer know that it's all down to the core temperature of the meat. Rare steak is 54°C [130°F], medium rare 57°C [135°F], medium 60°C [140°F] and well done 65°C [149°F]. The problem is that if you cook a steak the classic way, either under a grill [broiler] or in a frying pan [skillet], its temperature rises very fast so, to ensure the steak is cooked how you like it, you have to guess when to remove it from the heat. GUESSING! Do this too early and it will be underdone; a bit too late and it will be over.

Even if you manage to get it right, there is another problem you only discover when you slice your steak. Take a look! The doneness you want is only in the very centre. Between that and the crust, the rest of the meat (what I call the gradient) isn't right at all. My mission is to get rid of this gradient and have a perfectly cooked steak all the way through.

To do this, I use a cheat's controlled-temperature cooking technique called sous vide or – avoiding 'chef-speak' – vacuum packed and for this you need an ice box. This brilliant insulator is perfect not just for keeping food fresh but also for keeping it warm for a long time and, believe it or not, it's spot on for cooking steak. Something else you'll need is a digital meat thermometer, which you can pick up from a kitchen store or online fairly cheaply.

Now, take your nice thick steak and put it in a ziplock bag with a bit of butter and a sprig of thyme. Tuck the end of a straw into the bag alongside the steak and seal the bag so it is almost closed. Suck the air out through the straw, then remove the straw and seal the bag completely. As the bag is in close contact with the steak this will ensure more even cooking.

Fill the bath of the ice box with warm water. As the water will lose 1–2 degrees' heat per hour, I recommend that you have the water temperature slightly higher than the meat temperature you're aiming at. Put the sealed bag in the warm water along with the probe of the meat thermometer and close the box lid tightly.

From now it should take about 2 hours to cook your steak if it's 5cm [2in] thick or 1 hour if it's 2.5cm [1in] thick. Check the temperature displayed on the thermometer occasionally to make sure it's stable. If it needs adjusting, add a bit of hot water to the bath. The bigger the ice box, the more stable the temperature will be. The obvious but amazing consequence of cooking a steak like this is that the temperature cannot go higher than the starting temperature of the water, so the steak will never be overcooked. On the other hand, don't leave it in for more than 3 hours and when it's done, get it out of the bath.

When you remove the steak from the bag I admit it will look pretty miserable and lacking something crucial – a succulent, brown crust – but 1 minute on each side in a frying pan over a very high heat will soon fix that.

Slicing a steak cooked in this way is a thing of beauty. No gradient but beautiful pink meat, stretching from one caramelized crust to the other, that's incredibly juicy. There will be no going back...

Terrifyingly terrific steak tartare

OK, I know this dish isn't for everyone. Not only does it contain raw beef (as Italian carpaccio does) but also raw egg yolk (like homemade mayonnaise and proper chocolate mousse) so it comes with all the potential risks associated with those. This hasn't prevented me from making steak tartare at home from time to time. How come? I source the very best ingredients money can buy and, as my butcher is a close friend, he advises me on which meat to choose. So, does that eliminate all the risks? Nope, but I'm hooked. It's too good.

Serves 2

2 small gherkins [pickles]
1 Tbsp capers
1 small shallot
1 anchovy fillet
1 Tbsp each of fresh chopped parsley and chopped chives
100g [3½oz] highest-grade fresh sirloin steak, refrigerated
1 tsp each of mustard and tomato ketchup
a few dashes of Worcestershire sauce
sea salt flakes, freshly ground black pepper and a few drops of Tabasco
2 organic egg yolks

Finely chop the gherkins, capers and shallot and mash the anchovy fillet. Place in a bowl and mix in the chopped parsley and chives.

Take the steak out of the refrigerator and cut it into very thin slices, trimming off any fat or sinew. Stack the slices on top of each other and cut them into really small dice.

Add the diced steak to the bowl, along with the mustard, ketchup and Worcestershire sauce. Season with the salt, pepper and Tabasco. Mix everything together lightly but thoroughly. Divide in two.

Place a large, round cookie cutter, or just a piece of double foil folded into a ring (long live DIY!), on a serving plate and press one portion of the mixture into it to make a patty. Carefully remove the cutter or foil ring and place the egg yolk on top to serve.

VEGAN ALTERNATIVE?

Are you outta your mind? Probably, but try this. Leave out the egg and anchovy, add vegan mayonnaise, and replace the meat with a mixture of chopped cherry tomatoes, sun-dried tomatoes and red (bell) peppers, pretty tasty alternative, minus the muscle.

The beef bur-ger-nion

There is something truly wonderful about a mouthful of good burger. Crusty, soft, juicy, fresh, caramelized, salty, sweet, tangy... Every taste sensation bursts into life at the same moment. And, if you add a sauce made with red wine too, it's paradise.

Serves 1

½ carrot
a little juice from a jar of pickles
2 medium shallots
salt and pepper
oil
3 glasses of red wine
a pinch of sugar
1 beef stock [bouillon] cube, crumbled
1 tsp butter
1 tsp plain [all-purpose] flour
125g [4½oz] minced [ground] steak,
    shaped into a burger
1 rasher [slice] of bacon
3 button mushrooms
a drizzle of vinegar
1 burger bun, split in half
1 Tbsp mayonnaise mixed with
    a pinch of chilli flakes
1 lettuce leaf

Using a speed [swivel] peeler, peel the carrot and shave into thin slices. Put the slices in a small bowl and spoon over a little juice from your jar of pickles in your refrigerator. Set aside while you prepare the rest of the recipe.

Peel and slice the shallots into thin rounds. Set one or two rounds aside. Season the rest and add to a saucepan with a little oil. Fry for a few minutes over a medium heat. Add the wine, sugar and stock cube and season with pepper. Leave to reduce over a medium-low heat for 30 minutes, stirring from time to time. Thicken the sauce by mashing the butter and flour together until smooth and whisking this into the sauce. Bring to a gentle boil, taste and season with salt, if necessary. Cool and chill until needed.

Season the burger and brush on both sides with oil. Cook in a frying pan [skillet] over a high heat for 2–4 minutes on each side (depending on how thick it is). Remove from the pan and set to one side covered. Fry the bacon and mushrooms in the pan for a few minutes, remove, finely chop the mushrooms and set to one side. Add a drizzle of vinegar to the pan, stir to incorporate the juices sticking to the bottom of it and add this liquid to the wine sauce.

Quickly toast the burger bun and spread lightly with the spiced mayonnaise. Place the base of the bun on a plate or board and layer ingredients on top in the following order: lettuce leaf, burger, raw shallot slices, chopped mushrooms, 1 tablespoon of red wine sauce, bacon and pickled carrot slices. And more spiced mayonnaise if you like. Top with the lid of the bun.

Rare? No thanks... Most of the bacteria in a steak is on the surface, which is why, after the outside has been well seared, it is acceptable (indeed recommended) to eat the steak rare. But when it comes to a burger, the process of mincing the steak mixes the bacteria that was just on the outside all the way through the meat. Also, eating a burger rare will be like licking a piece of raw barbak. Yum. ('Barbak' is a slang word we French guys use for meat... I have to confess it's not very polite.) I will make an exception for steak tartare, though (page 114)...

Pulled pork hachis Parmentier

The purpose of this dish is to transform mashed potato and barbecue leftovers into something special. In fact, knowing how to make the most of leftover food is essential for anyone wanting to budget efficiently and, above all, not to waste any of the fresh produce they've chosen with such care.

Serves 4

400g [14oz] pulled pork or any
   another slow-cooked meat
2 red onions
2 garlic cloves
2 Tbsp oil
2 tomatoes, diced
1 Tbsp plain [all-purpose] flour
salt and pepper
1 egg, beaten
melted butter, for greasing
800g [1lb 12oz] mashed potatoes
100g [3½oz] tortilla [corn] chips,
   crushed into crumbs
50g [½ cup] grated cheese,
   e.g. Cheddar, Parmesan

Preheat the oven to 220°C/200°C fan/425°F/Gas 7.

Chop the meat into very small pieces. Peel the onions and garlic cloves and chop those as well.

Heat the oil in a frying pan over a medium-high heat and fry the onions and garlic for a few minutes. Add the diced tomatoes and the chopped meat.

Sprinkle over the flour and season with salt and pepper, if necessary (salt might not be needed if the meat has already been well seasoned). Stir to mix in the flour, turn down the heat to low and cook for about 10 minutes. Take the pan off the heat and stir in the beaten egg.

Brush an ovenproof dish with butter, spoon the meat mixture into it and cover with the mashed potatoes. Sprinkle the crushed tortilla chips and the grated cheese on the top. Bake for about 15 minutes or until the top is golden brown.

Just so you know...

'Hachis' is the French word for meat that has been minced or finely chopped and 'Parmentier' is the name of the guy who imported the first potato into France.

Meatballs done right

So, you think you can make a good meatball with only minced beef? Well, think again. It's all about getting the mix exactly right as you need to add pork, veal, bread, cheese... anything to make the meatballs juicy and melt-in-the-mouth. If you don't, not only will your meatballs be the same size as golf balls, they'll have the same texture as well and you don't want that, do you?

Makes about 20 meatballs

4–6 slices of white bread
milk
oil for frying
1 onion, very finely chopped
2 garlic cloves, crushed
400g [14oz] minced [ground] beef
150g [5½oz] minced [ground] pork
1 egg, beaten
50g [½ cup] finely grated cheese
   (pecorino or Parmesan)
flour for dusting

Serving suggestion
baguette
tomato sauce
fresh basil leaves

Dice the slices of bread, place in a bowl and pour over enough cold milk to cover. Soak until the bread is saturated and then squeeze out the excess milk. Heat a little oil in a frying pan over a medium heat, add the onion and garlic and fry until they are starting to brown.

Transfer the onion and garlic to a large bowl. Add the beef and pork, the bread, beaten egg and cheese. Knead well with your hands (if you don't fancy doing this, wear rubber gloves) – it is important to obtain a good, sufficiently damp, texture otherwise the meatballs won't work.

Shape the mixture into golf ball-size balls and dust them with flour. Heat oil in a frying pan and fry the meatballs in small batches over a medium-low heat. Allow about 20 minutes for this but, to double check the meatballs are done, cut one in half. It must be firm and cooked all the way through.

If you like, fill a small baguette with some of the meatballs, tomato sauce and basil, and tuck in.

Perfectionist or control freak?

Made this way the meatballs will flatten a little when you fry them but, for the perfectionists among you, if it's going to keep you awake at night (I feel your pain), you can ensure they remain perfectly round by poaching them first for a few minutes in a pan of simmering water.

Middle-kingdom roast chicken

This recipe pays tribute to Jamie Oliver's Empire Roast Chicken, which itself is a celebration of multicultural Britain. Hats off to you, Jamie!

Serves 4

For the five-spice powder
(Any leftover powder you make can be stored for several months in an airtight container away from light and heat. Also, I shouldn't say this but feel free to use a ready-made five-spice mix if you need to: better one that's done rather than none at all.)
1 Tbsp Sichuan peppercorns
5 whole star anise
1 tsp whole cloves
1–2 cinnamon sticks, depending on size
1 Tbsp fennel seeds

For the wet rub
4 spring onions [scallions], white and green parts separated
3 Tbsp neutral flavoured oil
2 garlic cloves, crushed
2.5-cm [1-in] piece of root ginger, grated
3 Tbsp light soy sauce
1 Tbsp rice vinegar or apple cider vinegar
1 Tbsp brown sugar

1.5kg [3lb 5oz] higher welfare chicken
1 tsp cornflour [cornstarch]
350ml [1½ cups] chicken stock
salt and pepper

For the five-spice powder, roast the whole spices in a dry pan over a high heat until they smell fragrant. Bash them to a powder with a pestle and mortar.

For the wet rub, finely chop the white parts of the spring onions and the green parts of two of the onions. Heat the oil in a pan over a medium-high heat and fry the chopped onions until golden. Strain, reserving the aromatic oil, and set the fried onions on kitchen paper [paper towels]. Mix the strained oil with the garlic, ginger, soy sauce, vinegar, sugar and 2 tablespoons of the five-spice powder to make a paste.

Cut deep slashes in the chicken legs and rub all over with three-quarters of the spice paste. If you wear rubber gloves to do this it's less messy but also less fun. (Oh, these sassy French.) Put the chicken on a plate, cover with clingfilm [plastic wrap] and marinate in the refrigerator for at least 2 hours. Remove from the fridge 30 minutes before cooking.

Preheat the oven to 200°C/180°C fan/400°F/Gas 6. Sit the chicken on a grill rack in a roasting pan, pour a glass of water into the bottom of the pan and roast for about 1 hour 30 minutes. While the chicken is roasting, put the remaining spice paste in a pan over a low heat. Mix the cornflour with the chicken stock and add to the pan. Bring to the boil, stirring, then simmer over a low heat until the mixture reduces to a syrupy sauce. Taste and season with salt and pepper.

Take the chicken out of the oven and push a knife into the flesh between the legs and the breast – the juice that runs out must be clear, not pink. If it is clear, the chicken is cooked! Cover it with foil and several tea towels [dish cloths] and leave to rest for 15 minutes. Serve the chicken with a flourish at the table, accompanied by the sauce. Finely slice the remaining green parts of the onions and sprinkle over the chicken with the fried onions.

Street lamb shish kebab

A kebab, bought and eaten in the street, conjures up extreme emotions. If it's well made, the combination of spices and grilled, juicy meat, will transport you to seventh heaven. If it's badly made, it will be an urgent invitation to the nearest loo. You can't get much more extreme than that.

Makes 6 kebabs

300g [10½oz] lean lamb, ideally from the leg
1 brown onion
215g [1 cup] natural full-fat yogurt
juice of 1 lemon
salt and pepper
1 tsp ground coriander
1 tsp ground cumin
1 tsp chilli powder
1 large tomato
1 green [bell] pepper
1 red onion

<u>Serving suggestion</u>
flat breads
yogurt
sliced chillies

Cut the lamb into flattened cubes (it's a brand new geometric shape, surely you know that?), about 2 x 2 x 1cm [¾ × ¾ × ½in]. Chop the onion and blitz with the yogurt, lemon juice, salt, pepper and spices in a blender until you have a smooth paste.

Spoon the lamb pieces and yogurt paste into a ziplock bag, seal the bag and mix and knead the two together. Leave to marinate in the fridge overnight or, failing that, for at least 2 hours, in which case knead the contents of the bag frequently (this makes up for the shorter marinating time).

Cut the tomato, green pepper and red onion into chunks the same size as the meat.

Thread the meat, tomato, pepper and onion alternately onto skewers and cook the kebabs on a griddle pan over a medium-high heat or, better still, grill them on a barbecue – 5–8 minutes should do it – turning them over from time to time.

Serve the kebabs with flat breads, yogurt and chillies. My mouth's watering just thinking about it.

Mussels marinière without the mussels

'Moules marinières', mussels cooked in a white wine and shallot sauce, is a classic French dish. It's tasty, cheap, cooks in less than 10 minutes and is totally sustainable - so let's do it. Except, let's not. Don't be square, that technique works fantastically well with any other small shellfish, like clams, for example!

Serves 2

5 shallots
2 garlic cloves
small bunch of fresh parsley
1 stick of celery
2–3 bay leaves
a few sprigs of fresh thyme
a few sprigs of fresh rosemary
1kg [2lb 4oz] fresh clams in their shells
1 Tbsp butter
about ½ bottle of acidic dry white wine, e.g. Muscadet, Sauvignon Blanc (or use a light beer or apple cider. If you don't want to use alcohol, add vegetable stock with a drizzle of vinegar instead – your dish will still be amazing)
salt and pepper
3–4 Tbsp double [heavy] cream

Finely slice the shallots and crush the garlic cloves. Remove the leaves from the parsley and celery stick, chop them and set aside separately.

Tie the parsley stalks, the celery stick (cut into shorter lengths), bay leaves, thyme and rosemary together in a bundle with cook's string. Scrub the clams with a small brush in plenty of cold water to remove any dirt or sand, discarding any that have broken shells or that are open and do not close when lightly squeezed.

Heat the butter in a very large saucepan and when it has melted, add the herb bundle first and fry for a minute or so to infuse it with the butter, and then add the shallots and garlic – the fresh herbs pimp and pump up the flavours of the dried ones. Fry until the shallots have softened, then add the wine (or whatever liquid you're using) and bubble so the wine reduces a bit. Season with salt and pepper.

Tip in the clams and celery leaves. Put a lid on the pan and cook until all the clam shells have opened, stirring once or twice. Discard any that remain tightly closed. The cooking time for the clams will depend on their size. Small ones (which taste so good) will open in 3–4 minutes; larger ones can take longer. Stir a couple of times while they cook to ensure those at the bottom don't open before the ones on top. When the clams are ready, I like to add a dash of cream. It's not classic, I know, but, honestly, I couldn't care less. Haha.

Remove and discard the herb bundle and then sprinkle in the chopped parsley. Pile the clams into serving dishes and ladle over the sauce. The flavours of the dish will be intense with the clams, shallots, butter and cream adding richness and the herbs freshness. Serve the clams on their own or with French fries on the side. And the rest of the bottle of wine.

Scallop carpaccio

I came across this scallop recipe while travelling through Northern Ireland and loved its simplicity, its rich and nutty taste and the fact that it used rapeseed rather than olive oil. Today, lots of people use olive oil in everything. It's certainly very good but I think: (1) its distinctive flavour doesn't work in EVERY dish and (2) there are lots of different and delicious oils out there just waiting to be discovered!

Serves 4

6 large sushi-grade scallops,
   corals removed
salt and pepper
1 lemon
3 Tbsp rapeseed [canola] oil
3 Tbsp chopped toasted hazelnuts
finely chopped fresh parsley sprigs

Cut the scallops horizontally into very thin slices, about 3mm [⅛in] thick. Season and divide the slices between 4 serving plates, overlapping them so they look nice.

Finely grate over a bit of lemon zest, but not too much, and squeeze over a little of the juice. Drizzle with the oil and scatter the hazelnuts and chopped parsley on top.

Serve at once.

Salmon, avocado and pickled beetroot rice bowl

This recipe is the ideal excuse for learning how to cook rice for sushi. It's also super-easy and looks great. So, what's not to like?

Serves 2

For the rice and seasoning
190g [1 cup] short grain rice
300ml [1¼ cups] cold water
75ml [⅓ cup] rice vinegar
50g [¼ cup] sugar
1 tsp salt

For the toppings
200g [7oz] sushi-grade salmon fillet, skinned
1 small pickled beetroot [beet]
1 avocado, peeled and pitted
¼ bunch of watercress
2 Tbsp salmon roe
a sprinkle of black and white sesame seeds

Put the rice in a fine-mesh strainer or colander and run cold water through it until the water runs clear. Transfer the rice to a rice cooker, add the measured water and cook the rice according to the manufacturer's instructions. If you like rice but you don't have a rice cooker (a bit hard to believe), go and buy one now.

Place a saucepan over a low heat, add the vinegar, sugar and salt and heat, stirring regularly, until the sugar and salt have dissolved.

When the rice is cooked, spread it out carefully in a large, deep dish so it will cool quickly, and spoon

the vinegar mixture evenly over it. Mix the rice gently with a spatula so you don't crush or break the grains. As soon as the rice has cooled, it's time to prepare the dish.

The rest is all about making it look good! Fill 2 serving bowls with the rice. Prepare the toppings by cutting the salmon, beetroot and avocado into thin slices. Divide the watercress into small sprigs, removing and discarding any yellow leaves and tough stalks. Arrange the salmon, beetroot, avocado and watercress sprigs over the rice and top each bowl with a tablespoon of salmon roe. Sprinkle with black and white sesame seeds. If you're rubbish at making things look pretty, go to Pinterest and check out 'Chirashi Bowl'.

For the recipe below, turn the page.

Fish fillet and tender vegetables in a rice wrapper

Cooking fish 'en papillote' (in a foil or paper parcel) conserves and even enhances all the flavours. The fish cooks slowly in the sealed parcel and the vegetables and herbs infuse its flesh. So far, so good, but the foil or paper wrapped around the fish is then thrown away. In my recipe, you can eat the wrapper as well. How come...?

Serves 1

3 rice wrappers
2 Tbsp grated white cabbage
2–3 mushrooms (depending on size), cut into thin strips
2 Tbsp bamboo shoots
175g [6oz] salmon or trout fillet, skinned
salt and pepper
a few sprigs of fresh coriander [cilantro]
1 tsp finely chopped root ginger
a few drops of sesame oil
a drizzle of olive oil
a drizzle of soy sauce

Soften the rice wrappers by dabbing them with a damp cloth or dipping them briefly in warm water. Place the wrappers on a board in a flower pattern so they overlap nicely.

Put the grated cabbage, mushrooms and bamboo shoots in the centre. Season the fish fillet well and place on top of the vegetables, then add some sprigs of coriander and some ginger. Drizzle over the sesame oil, olive oil and soy sauce. Fold the rice wrappers around the filling, making sure the packet is airtight.

If you don't have a proper steamer, it's not a problem – I don't have one either. So, DIY time! Screw up 3 sheets of foil into equal-size balls, each about the size of a clementine. Place these in a large saucepan and cover them three-quarters with water. Stand a small heatproof plate on top of the foil balls – the plate must not touch the sides of the pan. DIY steamer done! As an added bonus, it needn't only be used for fish in rice wrappers.

Rub the plate with a piece of oiled kitchen paper [paper towel] and then put the fish parcel on top. Cover the saucepan with a lid, place over a high heat and leave to cook for about 10–15 minutes.

Picture on page 129.

It's very important to remember:

Taste is not the only thing that matters in life. At the table, don't neglect either the presentation or the drama as it's the eyes that feast first.

An unforgivable French take on fish 'n' chips

You have to do it at least once: the best fish 'n' chips are eaten in the street in London, on a bench that's too narrow, surrounded by deafening car horns, in the pouring rain, with greasy hands and steamed up glasses. But, if that experience doesn't appeal, you can also cook fish 'n' chips at home.

Serves 4

For the sauce
2 garlic cloves, crushed
1 egg yolk
salt, to taste
1 tsp mustard
75ml [⅓ cup] neutral flavoured oil, e.g. rapeseed [canola], groundnut [peanut]
75ml [⅓ cup] olive oil
finely grated zest and juice of ½ lemon, plus extra lemon wedges to serve
pinch of chilli flakes

For the batter
225ml [1 cup] beer (I use a light or pale ale)
100g [1 cup] cornflour [cornstarch]
60g [½ cup] plain [all-purpose] flour
1 tsp salt
1 tsp pepper
2 Tbsp dried Mediterranean herbs, e.g. oregano, thyme, herbes de Provence
1 tsp bicarbonate of soda [baking soda]

For the fish
4 x 175g [6oz] fish fillets, about 1cm [⅜in] thick at the tail end and 2cm [¾in] at the top – you can use cod, haddock or another white fish. I even made the recipe once with monkfish and it was great but, whichever fish you choose, make sure you go for one with an MSC certificate.
cornflour [cornstarch] for dusting
groundnut [peanut] oil for deep-frying

For the sauce, put the crushed garlic, egg yolk, salt, mustard and lemon zest in a bowl. Mix the 2 oils together and gradually whisk in until incorporated. Bravo! You've made a mayonnaise. Finally, whisk in the lemon juice and chilli flakes.

For the batter, pour the beer into a wide, deep dish and lightly mix in the cornflour, flour, salt, pepper, dried herbs and bicarbonate of soda. Any lumps? Even better.

To prepare the fish, dust the fillets with cornflour until coated, shaking off any excess. Heat the oil for deep-frying in a large pan to 180°C [350°F].

Dip the fish fillets in the batter until coated, then deep-fry until golden brown. Drizzling a little extra batter over the fillets while they are cooking makes for even more crispy and crunchy shards of batter when fried. Drain the fillets on a plate lined with kitchen paper [paper towels] and serve at once with the sauce and wedges of lemon.

So, what happened to the chips? Answer: there aren't any. The fish is too good and anyway there is enough fat already. Instead, I suggest you accompany the fish with a crisp, full-flavoured salad.

Pictures overleaf.

Any fish, meunière-style

A dish that is very, very classic in French cuisine is 'sole meunière' (aka sole 'à la meunière', or – to translate – 'sole in the style of a miller's wife'). The fish is coated in flour before being fried in butter. It's easy and super-quick, plus – and not many people know this – lots of other types of fish can be cooked in the same way.

Serves 2

salt and pepper
2 trout, total weight about 700g [1lb 9oz], trimmed, scaled and cleaned (a job for the fishmonger!)
60g [½ cup] plain [all-purpose] flour
3 Tbsp neutral flavoured oil
80g [⅓ cup] butter
½ lemon
chopped fresh herbs (basil, parsley, tarragon...) for sprinkling

Season the inside of the trout with salt and pepper. Dust them in the flour until coated, then shake off any excess.

Heat the oil in a frying pan over a medium heat. Add the fish to the pan and when they are lightly browned underneath, add the butter. Fry for 4 minutes, still over a medium heat, until they are golden brown. Using a spatula, turn the fish over.

Lower the heat and cook for a further 5 minutes, spooning the oil and butter over the fish constantly and making sure the butter doesn't burn. Lift the trout out of the pan and onto serving plates.

Squeeze the juice from the lemon into the pan and whisk it into the hot, foaming butter and oil. Spoon over the fish, sprinkle with chopped fresh herbs and serve immediately.

Prawns in garlic, butter and parsley with Sichuan chilli oil

The aromatic oil, spiced with Sichuan pepper, is the real reason why I've chosen this recipe. It's easy, quick, fiery, spicy, full of flavour and you'll feel the pain, but it's also devilishly addictive. I find it fascinating to see how the aromatic profile of a dish can be changed completely with just a few drops of oil – don't you agree?

Serves 2 or 4 as a starter

For the chilli oil
(Prepare this at least 24 hours ahead)
225ml [1 cup] neutral flavoured oil
2.5-cm [1-in] piece of root ginger, peeled and sliced
white part of 4 spring onions [scallions], sliced
1 bay leaf
1 cinnamon stick
6 whole cloves
8 Tbsp red chilli flakes
1 Tbsp sesame seeds
3–4 Sichuan peppercorns

For the prawns
1 garlic clove
25g [1 Tbsp] butter
½ tsp salt
2 Tbsp chopped fresh parsley
225g [8oz] cooked peeled prawns [shrimp]
1 Tbsp neutral flavoured oil

For the chilli oil, heat the oil in a saucepan with the ginger, spring onions, bay leaf, cinnamon stick and whole cloves over a medium-low heat for about 5 minutes until the onions start to brown.

Strain the oil, return it to the pan and place over a medium heat. Meanwhile, put 5 tablespoons of chilli flakes in a heatproof ceramic or glass bowl. When the oil is just starting to smoke, pour half of it carefully over the chilli flakes in the bowl. Leave until the bubbles in the oil die down before continuing.

Add the sesame seeds to the bowl with another tablespoon of chilli flakes and the peppercorns. Pour in the remaining oil and leave to infuse for 24 hours, by which time the oil will have turned orangey red.

The oil can be kept in a covered container for a few weeks at room temperature or even longer in the refrigerator.

When ready to cook the prawns, crush the garlic with the butter and salt. Add the parsley and pound everything together. You might not know it but you've just made a true classic of French cuisine called *beurre maître d'hôtel* (see page 109). And that's all I'm saying.

Heat the oil in a frying pan [skillet] over a medium heat and fry the prawns for a few minutes until lightly browned. Add the garlic and parsley butter, stirring so the prawns are coated, and serve hot. It's already a very good dish but with a drizzle of the red oil, it's to die for.

Veggies

Baked caramelized miso aubergines

Although it's one of my favourite vegetables, the aubergine can be a capricious character in the kitchen. Badly cooked, it's tough, dry and bitter but, well cooked, it melts in the mouth, is juicy and almost sweet. By adding miso and caramelizing it, this hidden sweetness is emphasized even more.

Serves 2

2 aubergines [eggplants]
neutral flavoured oil
salt
1 vegetable stock [bouillon] cube
1 Tbsp soy sauce
2 Tbsp sake (or any dry white wine)
2 Tbsp mirin (or any sweet white wine)
2 Tbsp white miso
sesame seeds
chilli powder or chilli flakes, to garnish

Preheat the oven to 200°C/180°C fan/400°F/Gas 6.

Cut the aubergines in half lengthwise. Using a sharp knife, make deep diagonal cuts, 1cm [½in] apart, in the aubergine flesh, without piercing the skin. Now make more cuts on the opposite diagonal so the flesh is scored in a lattice pattern. Brush the flesh of each aubergine half with oil and sprinkle with salt. Lay the halves on a baking sheet, flesh side up, and cook in the oven for 35–40 minutes. Test with the point of a knife – the aubergine flesh should be very tender.

Meanwhile, put a saucepan over a high heat, add 125ml [½ cup] water, the crumbled vegetable stock cube, soy sauce, sake and mirin. Bring to the boil and bubble until the sauce reduces by one-third. Take the pan off the heat and add the miso, mixing it in well.

When the aubergines are cooked, brush them with the reduced mirin sauce, making sure you brush plenty into the cuts in the flesh. Sprinkle over some sesame seeds and grill [broil] the aubergines until the surface begins to caramelize and small bubbles appear on the surface. Remove the aubergines from the heat and sprinkle with a pinch of chilli powder or chilli flakes for that extra kick.

Something to meditate on

In France, a dish is considered complete (we say 'abouti') when nothing else can be added to it.
In Japan, a dish is 'abouti' when nothing can be taken away.
Which proves that it's all a question of your point of view...

Sexy ratatouille

Ratatouille is slow-cooked comfort food where the flavours of all the different ingredients combine harmoniously to produce a dish that is greater than the sum of its parts. The problem is that it can often look like vegetable porridge but not here, where it's guaranteed to blow you away!

Serves 4

4 large tomatoes
1 yellow courgette [zucchini]
1 green courgette [zucchini]
2 small aubergines [eggplants]
1 onion
2 red [bell] peppers, deseeded
2 garlic cloves
olive oil
sea [kosher] salt flakes and pepper
1 Tbsp chopped fresh thyme and
    rosemary leaves

Using a very sharp knife, cut the tomatoes, courgettes and aubergines into thin slices. As much as possible try to ensure all the slices are the same thickness so they cook evenly. Set the best-looking slices of the same size – at least 5cm [2in] in diameter – to one side for topping the ratatouille and keep the trimmings for the sauce.

Roughly chop the onion, peppers and garlic cloves. Heat 2 tablespoons of olive oil in a large frying pan over a medium heat and add the chopped veg to the pan with the sliced vegetable trimmings. Season with salt and pepper and add the thyme and rosemary leaves. Cook for 10 minutes and then blitz in a blender to make a thick, orangey red sauce.

Preheat the oven to 180°C/160°C fan/350°F/Gas 4. Brush an ovenproof dish with oil and spoon the sauce into it in an even layer, about 1cm [½in] thick.

Roll up your sleeves and arrange the reserved tomato, courgette and aubergine slices alternately on top of the sauce. So that they look really good, you need to overlap the slices quite tightly, a bit like the scales of a fish. Give the slices a final drizzle of olive oil and sprinkle over flakes of salt. Cover the dish with foil or baking parchment and bake for 30–45 minutes.

Place the dish in the centre of the dining table and wait for the "wow!" that is bound to follow. If it doesn't, take your dish back and eat the ratatouille in the kitchen all by yourself. But there's no chance of that!

An eye-opening mapo tofu (for vegetarians)

The day I discovered this recipe was the day I realized that Chinese cuisine had nothing in common with how we perceive it in the West. All I can say is that this recipe is a long way from chop suey, sweet and sour pork and crab wontons. And, as a not inconsiderable bonus, a large number of my YouTube followers in China have told me it's authentic...

Serves 2

300g [10½oz] silken tofu
2 Tbsp neutral flavoured oil
50g [1¾oz] mushrooms, minced
50g [1¾oz] onions, minced
1 heaped Tbsp dou ban jiang (a salty and pungent paste of fermented broad [fava] beans. If you can't find it, you could use Chinese soya bean paste, Korean gochujang or even Japanese red miso)
2 tsp dou-chi (fermented black soya beans)
2.5-cm [1-in] piece of root ginger, peeled and finely chopped
2 garlic cloves, finely chopped
white parts of 2 spring onions [scallions], finely chopped
1 Tbsp cornflour [cornstarch]

To finish
drizzles of sesame and chilli oils
green parts of 2 spring onions [scallions], finely chopped
a generous sprinkle of freshly ground Sichuan black pepper

Heat a wok or big pan of water over a high heat, bringing the water to simmering point. As the water is heating up, cut the tofu into 2-cm [¾-in] cubes. Add to the hot water, cook for a few minutes and then drain and set aside. This firms up the outside of the tofu.

Place a clean, dry wok over a high heat. Add the oil and then the mushrooms, onions and dou ban jiang.

Add the dou-chi, the ginger, garlic and white part of the spring onions and stir-fry until the ingredients give off a nice aroma. Pour 225ml [1 cup] water into a measuring jug and add two-thirds to the wok. Mix the cornflour with the remaining third until smooth and add it to the wok, stirring until thickened and smooth.

Add the tofu cubes but do not stir any more, simply push the cubes very gently back and forth in the wok so they don't break up.

Finish with drizzles of sesame and chilli oils, the finely chopped green parts of the spring onions and a generous sprinkle of freshly ground Sichuan black pepper. It's hot stuff!

The more you know...

The powerful but balanced taste of Mapo Tofu comes from its 7 fundamental taste sensations: 麻 « Má » (numbing), 辣 « là » (spicy heat), 烫 « tanhg » (fiery temperature), 鲜 « Xiān » (fresh), 嫩 « nène » (tender and soft), 香 « xiang » (aromatic) and 酥 « Sū » (flaky).

Polenta clafoutis

In France, a clafoutis is sweet. That's how it is, how it's always been and I see no reason to change that... except, of course, that it's fun! So, now clafoutis is savoury. There are no longer cherries but cherry tomatoes and it's goodbye baked custard and hello polenta! This 'trompe l'oeil' dish is delicious and dead easy to make. Another trick of mine? When it comes out of the oven, sprinkle it with basil leaves. It's classy.

Serves 4-6

1 litre [4 cups] whole milk
75g [½ cup] instant polenta
   [yellow cornmeal]
4 Tbsp grated Parmesan
1 Tbsp double [heavy] cream
salt and pepper
3 eggs, beaten
2 Tbsp roughly chopped basil leaves
250g [9oz] cherry tomatoes, halved

Preheat the oven to 190°C/170°C fan/375°F/Gas 5.

Bring the milk to the boil in a saucepan, add in the polenta and cook for 5 minutes, stirring occasionally. Stir in the Parmesan and cream and season with salt and pepper.

Cool a little and then stir in the beaten eggs, mixing well so the eggs do not scramble. Finally, stir in the chopped basil.

Pour the mixture into a wide, shallow ovenproof dish and top with the cherry tomato halves.

Bake for 35–40 minutes or until set.

Vindaloo – hot hot hot

This is far removed from the real deal but, if you like spicy curries, this is a super-easy weeknight supper. Vindaloo paste or powder is already hot but if you want even more fire, add red chillies as well. Just remember you can always add heat but once it's in, you can't take it out!

Serves 4

2 Tbsp neutral flavoured oil
2 onions, chopped
2 garlic cloves, finely chopped
2.5-cm [1-in] piece of root ginger, finely chopped
1 large or 2 small aubergines [eggplants], cut into 2-cm [¾-in] cubes
2 Tbsp vindaloo curry powder or paste
1 red chilli, finely chopped (or more, if you can stand the heat)
400-g [14-oz] can chickpeas [garbanzo beans]
400-g [14-oz] can chopped tomatoes
1 Tbsp tomato purée [paste]
1 vegetable stock [bouillon] cube

To finish
4 Tbsp natural yogurt
fresh chopped coriander [cilantro]

Serving suggestion
rice
naan bread

Heat the oil in a large saucepan and fry the onions over a low heat for 5 minutes or until translucent.

Add the garlic, ginger and aubergine cubes and fry over a medium heat for about 10 minutes until the aubergine turns golden, stirring from time to time so the cubes don't stick. Stir in the curry powder or paste and chilli and fry for another couple of minutes.

Drain and rinse the chickpeas and add to the pan with the chopped tomatoes and tomato purée. Dissolve the stock cube in 150ml [⅔ cup] hot water and add. Lower the heat and simmer for 15 minutes.

Divide the vindaloo between serving plates, top each with a tablespoon of natural yogurt and sprinkle over some chopped coriander.

Accompany with boiled or pilau rice and naan bread.

You wanna make your own garam masala spice mix to bring the flavour of this korma to the next level?

If so, here's a simplified recipe – toss 1 cinnamon stick, 1 tsp whole cloves, 1 Tbsp black peppercorns and 1 tsp black cardamom pods over a high heat in a dry frying pan until they smell toasty and aromatic. Transfer to a spice grinder or pestle and mortar and crush to a fine powder. Store in an opaque, airtight container.

Good karma korma

Even with my experience in the kitchen and my insatiable curiosity for other cultures, Indian cuisine is still very intimidating and difficult to simplify without betraying its roots. Multiple steps are involved to make the dishes, endless ingredients are needed and, above all, there is the delicate balance between the spices to get right. Here, I've done the work for you, so go for it...

Serves 4

For the nut and poppy seed paste
1 Tbsp poppy seeds
50g [1¾oz] whole blanched almonds
50g [1¾oz] unsalted cashew nuts

For the vegetables
2 large carrots
2 large potatoes, peeled
½ cauliflower
12 baby corn
225g [¾ cup] green peas

For the korma sauce
2 Tbsp ghee (clarified butter)
4 spring onions [scallions], finely sliced
1 Tbsp ginger and garlic paste (made by blitzing equal quantities of chopped root ginger and garlic with a little water until smooth)
2–3 mild green chillies, e.g. jalapeños, chopped
150g [¾ cup] natural full-fat yogurt
1 tsp ground turmeric
175ml [¾ cup] double [heavy] cream
1 tsp garam masala (see page 149 to make your own)

To finish
a few whole blanched almonds
a few unsalted cashews
raisins
chopped fresh mint and/or coriander [cilantro]

For the nut and poppy seed paste, pour boiling water over the poppy seeds, almonds and cashews and leave to stand for 30 minutes. Drain the seeds and nuts and blitz them to a smooth paste in a food processor, adding 60ml [¼ cup] water, if necessary.

For the vegetables, cut the carrots and potatoes into 2.5-cm [1-in] pieces, break the cauliflower into small florets and cut the baby corn in half. Set aside with the peas.

For the korma sauce, heat the ghee in a large frying pan, add the onions and fry until they are golden. Stir in the ginger and garlic paste and the chopped chillies. Turn the heat down to low, add the nut paste, yogurt and turmeric and stir until evenly combined.

Add all the vegetables, pour in 275ml [1¼ cups] water and stir well. Cover and leave over a low heat until the vegetables are cooked but not falling apart.

Take the pan off the heat and gently stir in the cream and garam masala.

Toast the almonds, cashews and raisins until the nuts are golden and scatter over the korma as a garnish. Finally, sprinkle with chopped mint and/or coriander.

Picture on pages 148–149.

The 5 essential kitchen knives you need

Chef + knife = love. This complex equation is the basis of the special relationship cooks have with the tools in their kitchen. Joking apart, having the right knives not only lets you work more quickly but also helps you feel more relaxed and comfortable in your kitchen. I've classified the knives I use in decreasing order of importance. P.S. If you're on a budget, concentrate on the first three...

Chef's knife

A 15-cm [6-in] blade is most practical; up to 22-cm [9-in] is more macho. For cutting, chopping, dicing and even breaking small bones, it is the ideal partner for all sorts of jobs in the kitchen. There's no point in spending a fortune but it is difficult to find a decent knife for less than 30 euros [about £25/US$40]. German, Japanese, American, French... it doesn't matter where it's made; choose one you feel comfortable using.

Paring knife

Smaller, with a blade about 10cm [4in] long, it complements the chef's knife perfectly, performing all those little tasks that require more precision, such as chopping a clove of garlic or lump of root ginger, as well as peeling a turnip or mushroom.

Serrated knife

There are certain foods that seem complicated or even dangerous to chop with a chef's knife. I am thinking of melon, watermelon, squash and things like that. So, rather than exerting brute force, with a serrated knife you only need to use a sawing motion. The knife is also very practical for cutting fragile foods and anything in layers, such as a sandwich, for example.

Filleting knife

A knife that has a long, thin and – most important of all – flexible blade. This is the Number One knife for removing the fillets from whole fish and for slicing ham and all other delicate, fragile foods super thinly. For me, I find the best ones come from Finland.

Chinese cleaver

Be aware that this is not the same as a meat cleaver but a lighter and much cheaper version. It is a knife with a very wide and quite heavy blade so you needn't worry about damaging it. I use mine for all kinds of things besides just preparing stir-fries – as a dough scraper, a worktop cleaner, a food shovel... oh, and I hack through big bones with it too.

Sweet!

Chocolate tart

You can recognize a good chocolate tart by the marks your teeth leave in the filling. It has to be dark, dense, rich and slightly sticky, with pastry that must be golden brown, not too thin but really crumbly. It's an intense experience and, for this reason, I never eat as much as I would, say, of an apple tart. Well, almost never.

Serves 6

For the pastry
175g [1½ cups] plain [all-purpose] flour, plus extra for rolling out
90g [⅓ cup] unsalted butter, diced and softened
1 Tbsp caster or granulated sugar
¼ tsp salt
1 egg, beaten

For the chocolate filling
150ml [⅔ cup] double or whipping [heavy] cream
200g [7oz] dark [bittersweet] chocolate, 70% cocoa solids, chopped
2 Tbsp butter, softened
a pinch of sea salt flakes

For the pastry, in a mixing bowl, rub the flour, butter, sugar and salt together with your fingertips until the mixture is like fine breadcrumbs. Add the beaten egg and gradually work it into the dry ingredients, kneading lightly to make a smooth dough.

Preheat the oven to 200°C/180°C fan/400°F/Gas 6. Roll out the pastry on a lightly floured board until 5mm [¼in] thick, and lift into a 20-cm [8-in] flan tin [tart pan] lined with baking parchment. Bake blind for 30 minutes until the pastry case is cooked (see page 70). Leave the pastry case to cool and then chill it while you make the filling.

For the chocolate filling, heat the cream in a saucepan over a medium heat. When bubbles start to appear on the surface, remove the pan from the heat. Put the chopped chocolate in a heatproof bowl and pour in the hot milk. Leave to stand for 1 minute – the time it will take for the chocolate to start to melt. Stir and then add the butter, stirring until the mixture is smooth and glossy. By the way, you have just made another French classic, a ganache – how about that?

Pour the mixture into the chilled pastry case and return to the refrigerator until the filling is firmly set. Sprinkle with a few sea salt flakes before serving.

SACRILEGE?

Just because most of the ingredients come from the supermarket doesn't mean this millefeuille will let you forget your manners. You don't eat a millefeuille layer by layer as that would be a betrayal of what the dessert is all about. Instead, you turn it gently on its side and cut across it with a knife and fork, so that each mouthful is a small sandwich of puff pastry and custard. Or, according to one French president, you eat it without any fuss using your fingers. #TheFrenchParadox

Millefeuille on the cheap

Millefeuille is a classic French pastry made by stacking three thin layers of puff pastry on top of each other, sandwiching them with crème pâtissière, and covering the top pastry sheet with icing. But I'm afraid I have to be honest - at the time of writing this recipe I have still never made puff pastry, crème pâtissière or icing - and I'm not going to start today.

Serves 8

1 rectangular sheet of ready-made puff pastry, measuring about 35 × 23cm [14 x 9in]
caster [superfine] sugar
thick vanilla custard or vanilla pudding mix (made up according to the packet instructions)
ready-made white icing and black icing

Preheat the oven to 200°C/180°C fan/400°F/Gas 6.

Unroll the puff pastry and lightly dampen the sheet with cold water. Prick it all over with a fork and dust with sugar. Carefully lift the pastry onto a baking sheet and place a wire rack on top to prevent the pastry puffing up as it bakes.

Bake the pastry for about 10 minutes or until it is golden brown.

Turn the pastry sheet over, moisten and dust with sugar. Replace the wire rack on top and return to the oven for a few minutes until the pastry has dried out and is lightly golden.

Using a serrated knife, cut the pastry into 24 small rectangles measuring about 4 x 8cm [1½ x 3½in] and spread 8 of the rectangles with a layer of vanilla custard or pudding about 1cm [⅜in] thick.

Place another rectangle of pastry over each of these, spread with thick custard or pudding as before and top with the remaining pastry rectangles.

Spread the top layers of pastry with the icings. You can create a beautiful marbled pattern by swirling the icings together, which is very traditional and means you'll be guaranteed entry into the exclusive club of top French *pâtissiers*. I'm joking. They will throw you out with the trash.

Tidy up and smooth the edges of the millefeuille with a knife.

Fake croissants and pains au chocolat

Makes about 6

2 sheets of ready-rolled all-butter
   puff pastry
icing [confectioners'] sugar
egg wash (1 egg beaten with
   2 Tbsp cold water)
flaked [slivered] almonds OR dark
   [semisweet] chocolate, cut into
   7.5-cm [3-in] sticks (2 sticks for
   each pain au chocolat)

What are you talking about? Me, make fake croissants?? (Sigh.) You must think I've completely lost it... On the other hand, they are not that fake, or rather no more so than my other little pastries, which I make with puff pastry anyway. They are also really cheap and super-quick to make. Whew, I'm not crazy after all.

Croissants

Preheat the oven to 220°C/200°C fan/425°F/ Gas 7.

Lay 1 sheet of puff pastry on a board and dust it with icing sugar (or, if you're feeling really decadent, spread with chocolate and hazelnut spread). Stack the second sheet on top – using 2 sheets of dough sandwiched together will give you a better rise in the oven.

Trim the pastry edges so the stack is roughly round and then cut it into wedges like a pizza.

Arrange a wedge so the tip is pointing towards you and, with both hands, roll it up slowly from the wide, rounded end, to make a croissant shape. Repeat with the other wedges and then lift the croissants onto a baking sheet lined with baking parchment.

Brush the croissants with egg wash and sprinkle with almonds, if you like. Bake for about 15 minutes or until puffed and golden brown. You can dust them with icing sugar or leave them plain.

Pains au chocolat

Preheat the oven to 220°C/200°C fan/425°F/ Gas 7.

Use the double puff pastry trick of stacking one sheet on top of the other (described opposite) and then cut the stack into 7.5 × 12.5-cm [3 x 5-in] rectangles.

Position one rectangle so a short side is facing towards you and lay a stick of chocolate across the pastry, 2.5cm [1in] from the top. Start rolling the pastry from the top: after one turn you won't be able to see the chocolate any more – that's good. Flatten the top of the roll gently with your fingers so it becomes oval-shaped. Give the roll a second turn, flattening it slightly again and place a second chocolate stick close to the roll. Give it a final roll and a last press, ensuring the join in the pastry is tucked underneath. Trim off any excess and repeat with the other rectangles and chocolate sticks.

Brush the pastry with egg wash and bake for 20 minutes or until puffed and golden brown.

Salted caramel

For me, it's the salt that makes this dessert so addictive. Not the sugar or the butter (the latter certainly helps but don't make me say something I didn't). With the salt, a balance is created and magic happens. If you think I'm going overboard, make the recipe and let's talk again.

Serves 2

100g [½ cup] granulated sugar
3 Tbsp unsalted butter
about 150ml [¾ cup] milk
a pinch of sea salt flakes

Put the sugar and butter in a frying pan [skillet] over a medium heat and sprinkle in a few drops of water. When the butter is completely melted, bring the mix to the boil (warning: it's mega mega hot) and cook until smooth, thick and caramel coloured.

Take the pan off the heat and mix in the milk to stop the mixture from over-cooking. Put the pan back over a low heat this time and stir gently until the mixture is the consistency you want. Using slightly less milk will give a spreadable texture; a little more and it will be like runny honey.

Add the pinch of salt. Transfer to a clean jar, leave to cool and store in the refrigerator. Use it on pancakes, in cakes, on tartines, stirred into yogurt, straight from the spoon...

"Thanks, Alex, you've ruined my saucepan..."

No need to panic. Just fill the pan with water, chuck in any sticky spoons as well and bring the water to the boil. Go and surf the web (in which case can I suggest a YouTube channel?) 'et voilà'. Without doing a thing your saucepan and utensils are clean again.

Drunk strawberries

This dessert is amazing. My mother used to make it when I was a child and – confession – I adored drinking the very cold, wine-flavoured syrup straight from the bowl. But don't panic: although it contains hardly any alcohol, the flavour of the red wine – refreshing, mature, spicy and tannic – is still very much there. Perhaps that helped develop my taste for good wine these days. Who knows?

Serves 2

½ bunch of fresh basil
3 glasses of red wine
100g [½ cup] caster or granulated sugar
½ tsp vanilla extract
250g [9oz] strawberries
freshly ground black pepper

Separate the basil leaves from their stalks.

Heat the wine in a saucepan over a medium heat, stirring lightly until it comes to a gentle boil. Add the sugar and stir until completely dissolved.

Continue cooking the wine until the smell of alcohol has disappeared (5–10 minutes). Turn off the heat under the pan and add the vanilla extract and the basil stalks. Set to one side.

Cut the strawberries into pieces and add to the wine mixture. Leave to cool and then chill in the refrigerator. When ready to serve, grind in one turn of black pepper from the mill and add a few basil leaves.

Which strawberries to choose?

The wine, the sugar and the vanilla all have very distinctive flavours so there's no point in buying small fragrant strawberries (plus they'll be overpriced). Much better to go for bigger strawberries that are deep red and will be very juicy, as the syrup will be better.

Sweet summer rolls

Picture the scene — mid-summer, blazing hot sun. Your small son pulls your arm and for the second time you drop a messy pulled pork and slaw sandwich. MMH. Not so sure that the sticky butterscotch buns planned for dessert are going to be any more successful. If only you'd thought of making my fresh sweet summer rolls...

Makes 10 rolls

100g [3½oz] dried rice noodles
100ml [⅓ cup] full-fat coconut milk
1 Tbsp runny honey
10 rice wrappers

Fruit, vegetable and fresh herb combinations that work well in the filling
EITHER mango, avocado and chopped mint
OR strawberries, red peppers and chopped basil
OR cucumber, pineapple and fresh chopped coriander [cilantro]

Serving suggestion
natural yogurt
runny honey

Cook the rice noodles according to the packet instructions. Drain and set them aside in a bowl. Mix in the coconut milk and honey.

Cut one-quarter of the fruit and vegetables you are using into attractive, thin slices (carpaccio, anyone?) and set these aside for decoration. Cut the rest of the fruit and vegetables into thin sticks – you are going to use these to fill the rolls.

Fill a large dish with warm water, dip a rice wrapper in the water and then place the wrapper flat on a board in front of you.

Put a few noodles and then some chopped herbs and fruit and vegetable sticks on top, laid horizontally, one-third of the way from the edge of the wrapper nearest your navel. Top with fruit and vegetable slices so they line up with the sticks.

Roll the rice wrapper around the filling, folding the sides in as you go to seal the summer roll. If you've done the job properly, you'll see the fruit and vegetable slices through the transparent wrapper.

Mix together some yogurt and honey and use as a dipping sauce for the rolls.

No-machine ice cream

I adore ice cream but I don't have an ice-cream maker. However, I do have a freezer so I make my ice creams in that. Logical – non?

Serves 4–6

For the ice cream
6 egg yolks
150g [¾ cup] caster or granulated sugar
225ml [1 cup] whole milk
450ml [2 cups] double [heavy] cream

Suggested flavourings
rum and chopped crystallized ginger
unsweetened cocoa powder
vanilla pods [beans] or vanilla extract
crushed strawberries

Place a large, thick glass or ceramic dish in the freezer to chill it thoroughly.

Put the egg yolks in a large bowl, add the sugar and mix until you have a smooth, pale yellow paste. This requires a bit of effort to make it smooth (electric hand whisk, maybe?).

Mix the milk and cream together in a saucepan, whisk in the egg yolk mixture and, stirring constantly, bring to a gentle simmer over a medium heat. On no account let it boil otherwise the egg yolks will scramble and you'll end up with some really weird ice cream.

Pour the mixture into the chilled dish and stir in your chosen flavouring until it is evenly mixed in.

Freeze for 1 hour. Take the dish out of the freezer and stir the ice cream briskly with a fork. Return it to the freezer for 2 hours. Remove the dish from the freezer and stir again briskly with a fork.

Return the ice cream to the freezer and freeze overnight.

Is it crystal clear?

A good ice cream is a smooth ice cream, that is to say its ice crystals are so small your teeth don't crunch on them when you eat it. Here, the speed at which you freeze the mixture is vital. Frozen slowly, without being stirred, the ice cream will produce large crystals that are hard and watery, whereas rapid freezing, combined with energetic stirring, will produce tiny crystals and thus a better ice cream.

Chouquettes (sweet puffs)

To tell the truth, I have a crush on this recipe and here's why – it's delicious and a real confidence booster as I always feel like a pastry chef at the end. The light, fluffy puffs are made with what the French call 'pâte à choux' – that means 'cabbage dough' in English. (Yum, I know). In fact, the name has nothing to do with cabbages. 'Choux' comes from the French word 'chaud', meaning warm, as the pastry dough is made over the heat. The more you know... The chouquettes are great split open and filled with ice cream, too.

Makes 30–40 puffs

For the dough
225ml [1 cup] milk and water,
   mixed in equal proportions
115g [½ cup] butter, diced
a pinch of salt
1 heaped Tbsp granulated sugar
115g [1 scant cup] plain [all-purpose]
   flour
3 eggs

pearl sugar nibs [nibbed sugar],
   or sugar cubes, bashed up into
   small pieces in a cloth

For the dough, put the milk and water, butter, salt and sugar in a saucepan over a medium-high heat. As soon as the butter and sugar melt and the liquid comes to the boil, tip in all the flour and mix over the heat with a wooden spoon until the dough comes together and dries out a little bit. It will form itself into a weird-looking ball that surprisingly won't stick to the sides of the pan.

Scrape out the dough into a bowl and add the eggs. Beat with the wooden spoon (or an electric hand whisk on low speed). To begin with, the dough won't come together but eventually it will. So, go for it, beating until you get a thick, glossy dough and muscles you can be proud of. The dough needs to hold its shape but not be too dry so add a drizzle of milk and mix a bit more, if necessary.

Preheat the oven to 200°C/180°C fan/400°F/Gas 6. Line a couple of baking sheets with baking parchment. If you've got a piping [pastry] bag, now's the time to use it. Otherwise, take a clean, strong plastic bag, turn it inside out and spoon the dough into it. Turn the bag back the right way, snip off one corner with scissors, and twist the top of the bag closed – hey presto, one homemade piping bag!

Pipe about 30–40 small puffs on the baking sheets, lightly pressing the points on top flat with your fingers. Sprinkle the puffs with pearl sugar nibs, gently pressing them into the choux. Bake the puffs for 20 minutes until they are golden. Transfer them to a wire rack to cool.

Tarte Normande

This tart from Normandy makes the most of locally grown apples and Calvados, which is apple brandy (Bourbon works a treat too). It's great both hot or cold and – if you're feeling brave – do as the Normans do and flambé the tart with extra Calvados before serving it.

Serves 6

For the pastry
175g [1½ cups] plain [all-purpose] flour, plus extra for rolling out
90g [⅓ cup] butter, diced and softened
1 Tbsp granulated sugar
¼ tsp salt
1 egg, beaten

For the filling
3–4 dessert apples, depending on size
2 eggs
90g [½ cup] caster [superfine] sugar
100g [1 cup] ground almonds
100ml [scant ½ cup] double [heavy] cream
4 Tbsp Calvados (or, if you don't want to use alcohol, fresh apple juice)
3 Tbsp flaked [slivered] almonds

For the pastry, in a mixing bowl, rub the flour, butter, sugar and salt together with your fingertips until the mixture is like fine breadcrumbs. Add the beaten egg and gradually work it into the dry ingredients, kneading lightly to make a smooth dough.

Roll out the pastry on a lightly floured board until 5mm [¼in] thick, and lift into a 23-cm [9-in] flan tin [tart pan]. Refrigerate while you prepare the filling.

Preheat the oven to 200°C/180°C fan/400°F/Gas 6. Put a baking sheet in the oven to heat.

For the filling, peel, core and quarter the apples. Cut each quarter into 3 wedges and arrange them in concentric circles in the pastry case. Beat together the eggs, sugar, ground almonds, cream and Calvados and carefully pour or spoon this mixture over the apples. Scatter over the flaked almonds.

Carefully lift the tart onto the hot baking sheet and bake for 30–35 minutes or until the filling is set and the tart is golden. Serve hot or cold.

Foolproof brioche

A word of warning – if you dislike fluffy buns, sweet buttery aromas, rich milky doughs and stretchy but obliging gluten, it's time to turn the page now. Otherwise, welcome to the wonderful world of brioche.

Makes 1 large brioche

500g [3½ cups] strong white bread flour
7g [1 tsp] instant yeast
2 eggs, beaten
200ml [scant 1 cup] whole milk, gently warmed (but not hot!)
2 heaped Tbsp granulated or caster sugar
1 tsp salt
100g [generous ⅓ cup] butter, diced and softened
extra butter and flour for the tin

In the unlikely event...

There is little chance of you having any left over the next day but, should that ever happen or you missed a bit first time round, on no account throw it away as it will make the best French toast in the world.

Sift the flour into the bowl of a food mixer and stir in the yeast.

Add the beaten eggs, milk, sugar, salt and finally the butter and mix on slow speed to begin with. When everything is evenly combined, increase the speed and continue mixing until you have a smooth dough that is soft and elastic but not too sticky.

Transfer the dough to a large bowl, cover with clingfilm [plastic wrap] and leave in a warm place for 1–2 hours or until it has doubled in size.

Punch the dough down and then knead lightly to burst any air bubbles inside. Divide into 3 equal pieces and roll each into a long, plump sausage. Brush a loaf tin [loaf pan] – the one I use is 30 × 13cm [12 x 5in] and 8cm [3¼in] deep – with melted butter and dust with flour. Plait [braid] the dough sausages together and then drop the plait carefully into the tin.

Cover with clingfilm and leave in a warm place to prove for about 15 minutes or until the dough just reaches the top of the tin. Meanwhile, preheat the oven to 200°C/180°C fan/400°F/Gas 6.

Bake the brioche for about 25 minutes or until well risen and golden brown.

Remove from the oven, turn the brioche out of the tin and leave to cool on a wire rack.

No-bake raspberry tart

This fantastic tart kills two birds with one stone – you make a cake without even lighting the oven, while passing for a French pastry chef in front of your friends. Hard to believe, eh? And, even better, I guarantee a round of thunderous applause when you place it in the middle of the table.

Serves 6–8

For the base
75g [generous ¼ cup] butter, melted
250g [9oz] digestive biscuits [graham crackers], blitzed into crumbs

For the crème pâtissière
400ml [1¾ cups] whole milk
3 eggs
90g [½ cup] caster [superfine] sugar
4 Tbsp plain [all-purpose] flour
1 tsp vanilla extract

For the topping
250g [2 cups] raspberries, defrosted if frozen
4 Tbsp seedless raspberry jam

For the base, stir the melted butter into the biscuit [cracker] crumbs and press over the base and 4cm [1½in] up the sides of a 20-cm [8-in] springform cake tin [cake pan]. Refrigerate to firm up while you make the crème pâtissière.

Heat the milk in a saucepan until bubbles appear on the surface. While the milk is heating, beat the eggs, sugar and flour together in a jug until smooth. Pour a little of the hot milk into the egg mixture, stir well and then pour back into the pan. Stir constantly over a medium heat until the custard is thickened and smooth. Make sure you keep stirring vigorously all the time or lumps will form and you don't want that! If this starts to happen, take the pan off the heat and beat or whisk the custard until it is smooth again.

Take the crème pâtissière off the heat and stir in the vanilla extract. Tip into a bowl and press clingfilm [plastic wrap] over the surface to prevent a skin from forming. Leave until cold and then spread in the chilled tart case.

For the topping, cover the crème pâtissière with the raspberries. Heat the jam with 1 tablespoon of water in the microwave until it bubbles and brush it over the raspberries. Chill the tart until ready to serve. Release from the tin and carefully slide onto a serving plate.

One-pot yogurt cake

Hey – the great thing about this cake is you don't need any scales or cups to measure out the ingredients, just the pot you bought the yogurt in. So how easy is that? And did I mention that it's absolutely delicious as well? But don't take my word for it, try it yourself.

Makes 1 small cake

oil for greasing the loaf tin
1 pot of natural yogurt (about 150g [5oz])
2½ pots of plain [all-purpose] flour
1½ pots of caster or granulated sugar
1 tsp vanilla extract
finely grated zest of 1 lemon
3 eggs, beaten
½ pot of sunflower oil
1 tsp baking powder

Preheat the oven to 180°C/160°C fan/350°F/Gas 4. Grease a small loaf tin [pan] by brushing it with oil and line the base and sides with baking parchment.

Scrape the yogurt out of the pot into a mixing bowl. Wash and dry the pot and use it to measure the other ingredients. Add the flour, sugar, vanilla and lemon zest to the bowl and stir until combined. The mixture will not be smooth at this stage – it will look quite dry and crumbly.

Add the beaten eggs, stir well, then add the oil and baking powder. Beat or whisk until the mixture is glossy, smooth and doesn't have any nasty lumps left in it.

Scrape the batter out of the bowl into the loaf tin. Bake the cake for 30–35 minutes or until it has risen, is golden brown and a cake tester or skewer pushed into the centre of the cake comes out clean with no uncooked batter sticking to it.

Cool the cake in the tin for 10 minutes before turning it out onto a wire rack to cool completely.

6 magical microwave winners... and 1 epic failure

Some people see it as the devil's work but, for me, a microwave is just a useful extra piece of equipment in the kitchen. It's pretty effective, I have to say, but you have to know how to use it. Here are a few microwaving tips and tricks that you might not be aware of.

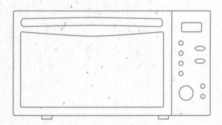

Instant cake

Mix some self-raising [self-rising] flour with a bit of milk, a beaten egg, salt and sugar until you get something like a thick pancake batter. Pour into a mug so it's one-third full and microwave on full power for 1 minute and then in 30-second bursts until done. Instant cake!

High-speed cooking

Artichokes take 45 minutes to cook, but only 8–10 minutes in the microwave. I also frequently pre-cook potatoes before I roast them. Put the potatoes in a bowl, add 2–3 tablespoons of water, cover and microwave on full power for 8–10 minutes until just tender when pierced with a knife. Finish in a hot oven.

Even heating

Placing a dish in the centre of the microwave turntable is disastrous, as your food will be burning in some places and frozen in others. Place the dish at the edge of the turntable.

Crisps [potato chips]

Put very thin, even slices of potato in a dish and cover with microwave-safe clingfilm [plastic wrap], or – as I prefer to do – very lightly coat them in oil and place them directly on the glass microwave turntable (if you do this you'll have to separate them with a spatula). Cook for 2½ minutes on full power and then in 30-second bursts until crisp. They should take 3–5 minutes in total.

Worry-free garlic

To save time when you have to peel a lot of garlic, microwave a whole bulb for 20 seconds and then take it out without burning yourself. Rub the bulb between your hands to separate the individual cloves and remove their skins. And, there's even more magic, as the smell on your fingers will last FOREVER!

Chopping without tears (almost)

Peel an onion, make a couple of small cuts in it so it doesn't explode (oh, the joys of cooking!) and microwave for 30 seconds. This releases the tear gases so the task of chopping the onion will be much less traumatic.

Something you must never do

Twice in my life I've tried to hard-boil an egg in the microwave. Twice it has exploded, ruined the inside of my oven and the smell in my kitchen has been unbelievable. TWICE!

Index

Acknowledgements

Let me shout a big "merci" to all of those without whom this cookbook would have been nothing but a distant project: Chetna, Stuart, Céline, Emily, Dan, Wendy, Becks, Becci, Alex and everyone at Quadrille.

A special mention to Jamie Oliver, Donal Skehan and Jacques Pépin for those (very) kind words.

Legit credits to all my family for being so supportive, cheerful when I need it, always there for me ♡

Lovely hug to my wife and a final cheeky high five to Sacha, my man.

Published in 2018 by Quadrille,
an imprint of Hardie Grant Publishing

Quadrille
52–54 Southwark Street
London SE1 1UN
quadrille.com

Cataloguing in Publication Data:
a catalogue record for this book is available from the British Library.

Text © Alexis Gabriel Aïnouz 2018
Photography © Dan Jones 2018
Design © Quadrille 2018

Reprinted in 2018
10 9 8 7 6 5 4 3 2

ISBN 978-1-78713-223-8

Printed in China

Publishing Director Sarah Lavelle
Commissioning Editor Céline Hughes
Art Direction and Design Emily Lapworth
Cover Lettering Arielle Gamble
Photographer Dan Jones
Prop Stylist Alexander Breeze
Food Stylist Becks Wilkinson
Food Stylist (cover and pages 33, 125 and 169) Rebecca Woods
Assistant Food Stylists Joseph Railton and Jo Jackson
Translator and Copy-Editor Wendy Sweetser
Production Controller Tom Moore
Production Director Vincent Smith